· Wiltshire Place Names ·

· Wiltshire Place Names ·

compiled by

Richard Tomkins

Red Brick
PUBLISHING
1983

Redbrick Publishing
38 Overbrook
Swindon
Wiltshire

First published 1983

ISBN 0 9507182 5 4

Typesetting and origination by
Alan Sutton Publishing Limited.
Photoset 10/11 Bembo
**Printed in Great Britain by Dotesios
(Printers) Ltd., Bradford-on-Avon,
Wiltshire.**

· ambrosia Ambrosio ·

Contents

Introduction

Britain's landscape first began to be inhabited and exploited by man to a significant degree during the Neolithic period, from about 4500 BC onwards. Neolithic man, living in primitive pit dwellings, built simple earthen circles to harbour his family and cattle from attack by savage beasts and raiders. Monuments such as Avebury and Stonehenge date from these pre-Christian millenia, vivid reminders of the Bronze Age way of life and pointers to the genius inherent in an otherwise backward society. For, despite the many striking iconic achievements within the Wiltshire landscape, progress in other spheres of Neolithic life was painfully slow. Innovation and invention took centuries to penetrate the deep forests and wild uplands of southern England, and the primitive lifestyle of the tribal regimes changed little until the advent of the Iron Age, which brought with it the migration of Celtic peoples from Europe, from the 5th century BC onwards.

Somewhere within these shadowy years of pre-history lie the beginnings of our language and the origins of the earliest place-names; names which in the ensuing ages have been subject to modification, enrichment, adaptation — and often replacement — by wave upon wave of settlers to this country's shores. Thus to understand the origin of names, it is important to set them within a broader historical framework: to view them against the backdrop of a complex process which started in the Stone Age, continuing through Celtic, Saxon, Danish and Norman times, to the present day.

When the Romans first arrived in southern Britain in AD 43, they stepped ashore upon an untamed and dangerous island inhabited by a number of understandably hostile Celtic tribes. During the preceding four centuries of their occupation, the Celts — a people of warriors, tribesmen and farmers — had made a considerable impact upon the face of the country. A more intensive system of farming and land enclosure had been adopted, while a sophisticated approach to fortress building had resulted in a network of hilltop defence stations, most of which remain today as striking memorials of the British people. The formidable earthworks of Yarnbury Castle, near Wylye, and the prominent Figsbury Ring, near Salisbury, are both examples of Iron Age fortresses.

The Roman aim was to subdue the islanders and produce a unified state by means of a republican system of law and government and the introduction of a unifying language, Latin. Ultimately, the British were to become Romanised but, due to the decline and eventual collapse of the Empire, never completely Roman. The indigenous tongues, too, became modified during the period of Roman domination, but never died out — indeed, as the Welsh, Gaelic and Breton languages, they have survived for many more centuries. Numerous place-names also retained their original Celtic elements, with Latin names often incorporating older roots. At least two settlements in Wiltshire are mentioned in Roman Itineraries, the names of which both have strong Celtic elements: *Sorbiodonum* (Old Sarum) and *Cunetione* (Mildenhall) include pre-Roman words which describe a river and a hill-fort respectively. The enduring nature of the Celtic language is noted particularly in the names of rivers, hills and other natural features.

As the Roman Empire began to age and die, Britain's position as a stronghold grew weaker and weaker, until once again it lay ripe for colonisation by tribes from across the North Sea. During the 5th century AD, barbarians, mercenaries and other — more peaceable — Anglo-Saxon settlers began a steady influx into Britain. With them they imported a new societal framework, a new pattern of settlement and a new language — English — which was to provide the basis for our present-day tongue.

In the north and east of the country, the sub-Roman population offered little effective opposition to this Saxon folk movement, but in Wessex and the south-west peninsula an organised resistance movement appears to have sprung up under legendary British supremos such as Ambrosius and Arthur. Although the history of the Dark Ages is sketchy, there is evidence that part of the British strategy involved the re-occupation of many Iron Age hill-forts and the construction of a huge palisaded ditch, the Wansdyke, to ward off the Saxon advance; this they successfully managed until the latter half of the 6th century. The Romano-British forces trounced the invaders in the celebrated battle of *Mons Badonicus* (probably Liddington Hill, near Swindon), and also led several successful campaigns against the newcomers. But with crucial Saxon victories at Old Sarum in AD 552 and at Barbury four years later, the last pockets of British resistance finally crumbled. By the start of the 7th century, Wessex had become a Saxon kingdom.

With the onset of peace, the way was open for the Saxon folk to settle, without fear of war, in small tribes and extended families. Pioneer settlements were probably temporary, the peoples leading a semi-nomadic life until such time as they found a site which they considered suitable for permanent settlement. Thus the earliest tribal bases were known simply by the name of the particular tribe: in Wiltshire there is only one definite example of an early tribal name. This is All Cannings, a name derived from OE *Caningas*, meaning 'the people of Cana'. More common is the tribal name with a suffix attached, descriptive of the type of permanent settlement which had been founded, or indicative of its position in the landscape, e.g. Durring-ton, Manning-ford, Beeching-stoke. Durrington, for example, denotes an enclosure or farmstead founded by members of the *Dyring* people.

The Anglo-Saxons were first and foremost home-lovers. Their language gives important clues about their attitudes towards land and property, for the commonest place-name elements reveal the importance of fortifications, enclosures and private settlements. Giving credence to the maxim that 'an Englishman's home is his castle' are place-name suffixes such as *-tun*, *-ham*, *-worth*, *-stoke*, *-burh* and *-wick*. All denote enclosures of some sort, and are common in Wiltshire as throughout southern England. By far the most widespread element is OE *-tun*, used generally to describe an enclosure or settlement and later applied more universally to villages and towns. Saxon names are frequently descriptive of the immediate topography, and it is important to interpret them in environmental terms. Fieldwork confirms that names are often still accurate today: Netheravon, Oare and Winterbourne, for example, all provide valid contemporary descriptions of settlement sites.

By the 8th century the Saxons were pursuing a programme of land clearance and cultivation, involving a gradual contraction of lowland forest cover to allow the creation of open fields, enclosures and meadows. The growth in farming was followed by a significant upturn in national and international trade, which led indirectly to the establishment of markets and fairs in hundreds of places throughout England.

Along with the market, the other focal point of rural life was to be the village church. With the re-introduction of Christianity to Saxon England and the foundation of an ecclesiastical framework, monasteries, abbeys and churches began to feature regularly in place-names. However, many poorer settlements at first only had a stone or wooden cross about which local people would gather for worship, as evidenced for example by the names of Christian Malford, Rood Ashton and Bishopstrow.

From the early 9th century the next wave of invaders, the Danish Vikings, began to harry the British Isles from the south and east. In 874 the Midland kingdom of Mercia fell to the assailants, and by 878 a sizeable Danish army had advanced into Wessex from Gloucester. A camp was established at the stronghold of Chippenham, whence the Danes set about plundering the surrounding areas. In reply, the Saxon forces under King Alfred (848–899) advanced from the cover of Selwood Forest, gathered support at *Ecgbryhtesstan* (probably Brixton Deverill), and marched forward to encounter and defeat the Danes in a major battle at Edington. Guthrum, the Danish king, was subsequently baptised a Christian, and a peace treaty, *Danelaw*, was formulated under which the Danish occupation was restricted to lands north of the Thames. The threat of hostilities evidently remained, as Alfred was prompted to bolster the defensive system of Wessex by the construction of a chain of fortified *burhs* (in Wiltshire, these were at Cricklade, Malmesbury, Chisbury and Wilton). Another of Alfred's major innovations, this time a literary one, was the Anglo-Saxon Chronicle, a vast documentary record of important events in Saxon England. The Chronicle was instituted in the 9th century, continuing until 1154, thus providing valuable source material for the interpretation of historical and etymological developments during this period.

Although Britain was to experience a generation of Danish rule during the early 11th century, it was the Normans who were ultimately to conquer the country once and for all under King William in 1066. Unlike the gradual Saxon occupation some 500 years previously, the Norman Conquest took the form of a swift military coup (insofar as a five-year struggle may be termed 'swift'!). Cunliffe describes it as "the imposition of an aristocracy on native peasants" for, despite their minority, the Normans soon became the principal landowners and holders of all positions of power in the country. A new language, French, was introduced, although documents, charters and major literary works such as the Domesday Survey, were written in Latin (English remained in currency, but was 'unfashionable' amongst the Normans). Compiled in 1086 as a general assessment of property and ownership, Domesday provides vital evidence about the nature of settlement in England at the time of the Conquest, and is the earliest comprehensive gazetteer of place-names.

Many Norman families migrated to England in the wake of King William. Their names, or those of their home towns in Normandy, were often appended as feudal and manorial suffixes to existing place-names, wherever the families settled or were granted land by the King. Milton Lilbourne, Berwick Bassett and Fifield Bavant are three examples of so-called duplex names. Latinised additions, usually in comparative forms such as *Alta*, *Nether* and *Magna*, *Parva*, were also given to names, although these were used primarily by scribes and rarely entered the spoken language; for the purposes of documentation, a name such as Donhead St Mary would be rendered as *Donhead Sancte Marie*, while Highworth became *Alta Worth*. A few Latinised names survive today: Hinton Parva and Stratford-sub-Castle are instances. The Church, as in later Saxon times, continued to exercise a considerable influence on etymology, with various suffixes indicating church dedications, monasteries, priories and the holdings of abbots and abbesses.

Until the introduction of printing in the 16th century, spellings of place-names varied wildly, although pronounciation in general remained remarkably consistent from one century to the next. Words written depended largely on the writer's interpretation of the spoken word, which is perhaps why even a simple name such as Huish could produce such variants as *Iwis*, *Hiwis*, *Huwes*, *Hywysshe*, while remaining phonetically the same over a 300-year period. Some names have undergone complete changes, such as Maiden Bradley, which was formerly known as *Deverill*, and Maddington, which appeared as one of the many *Wintreburnes* in the Domesday Survey. At the other end of the spectrum is a name like Stapleford, spelled exactly the same today as it was in 1086.

No general rules can be applied to the evolution of names since Domesday, and factors such as dialect, abbreviation and error all play their part in determining the exact form that a name finally takes. Structurally, the development of Wiltshire place-names was complete by about the 16th century, since when only minor alterations in spelling, pronounciation and synthesis have taken place.

Guide to the Book

Place-names are listed alphabetically. For example:–

Bowerchalke (Bower Chalke) (burchalk) S.W. of Broad Chalke

The heading gives firstly the complete place-name, any alternative spelling (Bower Chalke), any local pronounciation (burchalk), and finally the place's approximate position on the county map, which is found on page 14.

Beneath the heading are listed the significant spellings and alternative forms of the place-name during the years, with dates. Where exact dating is not possible, the reigning monarch's name is given instead, e.g. *Hen.II* denotes that the particular reference dates from the reign of Henry II, 1154–1189. All dates are *anno domini*, unless otherwise specified in the text, which gives where possible a full explanation of the name and any other relevant information. Cross-references are given by capital letters. For documentary sources and a more comprehensive historical listing of names, the reader is referred to the English Place-Name Society's excellent volume on Wiltshire.

Main abbreviations are as follows:–

DB	Domesday Book (all references dated *1086* are from this source)
OE	Old English
ME	Middle English
WS	West Saxon
c.	century
c	circa

Although basically a digest of existing source material and published works, there are bound to be certain errors and omissions in this volume, for which the author takes full responsibility. The publishers will be grateful to receive any corrections, additions or suggestions for inclusion in possible future impressions of the book.

Common OE elements found in Wiltshire place-names

Approximate meanings are given. A more precise meaning of a particular name can often be given in the text if there is sufficient evidence. Examples of place-names which incorporate the elements are given in brackets.

ærn	dwelling, household (Chitterne)
beorg	hill, barrow, burial mound (Brokenborough)
berie, beria	open field (Avebury)
broc	brook (Beversbrook)
brycg	bridge (Bulbridge)
burh, byrig	fortified place (Alderbury)
burna	stream (Aldbourne)
cot, cote, cotan	cottage, group of cottages (Coate)
cumb	combe, small chalkland valley (Boscombe)
denu	valley (Chiseldon)
dun	down, hill (Downton)
feld	field, open space (Chalfield)
ford	ford, river crossing (Axford)
ham	home, homestead (Bremilham)
hamm	enclosure, place enclosed by water (Bremilham)
ham-tun, hampton	home-farm, farmstead (Bathampton)
healh	corner of land (Ludgershall)
heall	hall, palace, residence (Bincknoll)
hid	hide, a measure of land (Fifield)
hyll	hill (Hill Deverill)
lade, gelade	way, passage (Cricklade)
leah	meadow, clearing (Ashley)
mære	boundary, mark (Buttermere)
stan	stone (Hodson)
stoc	settlement, stockaded place (Baverstock)
tun	farmstead, enclosure (Abbotstone)
weorth	homestead, small farm (Atworth)
wic	grange, dairy farm, outlying farm (Berwick Bassett)
wielle	well, spring, stream, river-source (Crudwell)
wudu	wood, forest (Bowood)

Thanks

I acknowledge the help given by the English Place-Name Society in the preparation of this book, and my thanks are due for permission to incorporate certain material from the Society's publication on the Place-Names of Wiltshire. Grateful thanks also to the Wiltshire Library & Museum Service, from whose collection at Swindon Divisional Library I have loaned illustrations for inclusion in this volume. The illustrations of Avebury and Stonehenge are taken from Stukeley's *Abury*, and those of Old

Sarum from Hoare's *Ancient Wiltshire*. Acknowledgements to Don Hampshire of Stanton St Bernard, who supplied information on local pronounciations, and Sue Winward, who checked the proofs.

Bibliography and authors referred to in the text

John. C. Longstaff	Notes on Wiltshire Names (Library Press 1911)
Ralph Whitlock	Historic Forests of England (Moonraker Press 1979)
Barry Cunliffe	The Making of the English (BBC 1973)
Rev W.H. Jones	The Names of Places in Wiltshire
Gover, Mawer & Stenton	The Place-Names of Wiltshire (Cambridge University Press 1939)
Einar Ekblom	The Place-Names of Wiltshire (1917)
E. Ekwall	Studies in English Place-names (1936)
George Osborn	Exploring Ancient Wiltshire (Dorset Publishing Company 1982)
Michael Wood	In Search of the Dark Ages (BBC 1981)

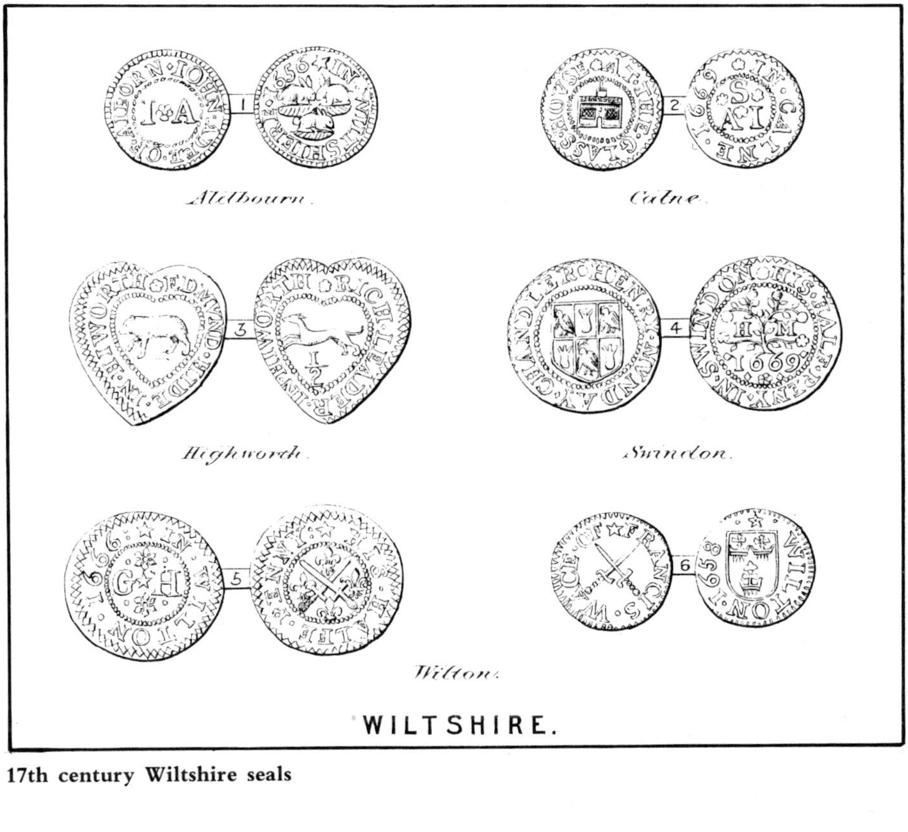

17th century Wiltshire seals

Map of Wiltshire

Showing main settlements, rivers and forests

Gazetteer

Abbotstone (abbeston) E. of Downton
1249 Abbedeston *1272 Aboteston* *1322 Abbesseton* *1405 Abbeston*

Originally OE *abbodes-tun*, or 'abbot's farmstead'. The estate was held in 1339 by the Abbess of Wilton, and the name changes from *Abbot-* to *Abbess-* accordingly.

Ablington N. of Amesbury
1086 Alboldintone *1249 Eblinton* *1487 Ablyngton*

This name derives from OE *Eadbealdinga-tun*: 'the farmstead of the descendants or tribe of Eadbeald'.

Aldbourne N. of Ramsbury
880/5 æt Ealdincburnan *1086 Aldeborne* *1181 Aldiburna* *1217 Audiburne* *1226 Audingeburn'* *1347 Oldeborne* *1428 Aldebourne*

Eald is WS 'old' and possibly the first element is a personal name, *Ealda* ('old one'). Alternatively, the complete name means 'old stream', with reference to the smallness of the river here.

Alderbury S.E. of Salisbury
972 Æthelware byrig *976 Ædeluuaraburh* *1086 Alwaberie, Alwaresberie* *1195 Ailwardesberie* *1288 Alwardesburi* *1341 Alrebury* *1476 Alewardbury*

Judging by the earliest form, the name evidently means 'Æthelwearde's fortified place': *byrig* is the dative singular of OE *burh*, a case commonly found in old charters and documents. *Burh* was a word applied to prehistoric earthworks, Iron Age camps and later Saxon defensive works. For the confusion of *burh* with *berie* (OE 'open field'), see AVEBURY. The personal name is a woman's.

Alderton N.W. of Grittleton
1086 Aldritone 1249 Aldrynton 1426 Alderyngton 1675 Aldrington

'Ealdred's farmstead'. *Ealdred* was a common OE personal name, in this instance a local Saxon landowner.

All Cannings E. of Devizes
1086 Caninge c1100 Caneganmersc 1139 Canenghis 1166 Chaninges 1186 Kaninges 1205 Aldekanning 1256 Eldekaninges 1268 antiqua Caninges 1283 Alecaninges 1306 Allescannyng 1428 Allecanynges

Probably one of the oldest Saxon names in Wiltshire, Cannings is derived from an early tribal name, *Caningas*, ie. 'the people of Cana'. This is indicative that the name was in use even before the village itself was established, when only a nomadic community existed. Many similar place-names of later origin will have a suffix such as *-ton* or *-don* attached (eg. DURRINGTON and CLARENDON), and these date from the time when a particular tribe first settled in a permanent spot. The original name of Cannings included nearby BISHOP'S CANNINGS. Caen, or Cane, Hill in the locality derives from the same source. It is recorded that the Danes penetrated as far as *Caneganmersc* (Cannings Marsh) from the north-west after the burning of Northampton in the early 11th century. The Marsh occupied the low-lying land to the east of Devizes, and was drained during the Middle Ages. ALLINGTON and BEECHINGSTOKE were both in Cannings Marsh. The prefix 'All' is probably from ME *eald* ('old', as in ALDBOURNE). Coincidentally, the parish church is dedicated to All Saints.

Allington S.E. of Amesbury
1086 Allentone 1242 Aldington 1270 Alletona 1316 Aldynton

'Ealda's or Ælla's farmstead': see ALDBOURNE. Longstaff mentions a Saxon tribe called the *Ælings* in connection with the village.

Allington N.W. of Chippenham
1086 Alentone 1289 Alyngton 1316 Alynton 1397 Alyngtone

See ALLINGTON, above.

Allington N.E. of Devizes
1086 Adelingtone 1242 Athelinetona, Alungeton 1275 Alington 1341 Alyngton 1394 Alyngton in Canyngmershe

If the DB form is to be trusted, the name is *Æthelinga-tun* or 'Æthel's farmstead'. However, the proximity of ALL CANNINGS suggests that the first element is the name *Eald*. See also ALLINGTON, above.

Alton N. of Amesbury
1086 Eltone 1270 Alletona 1310 Aleton 1428 Alton

'Ælla's tun or farmstead'. See ALLINGTON, above.

Alton Barnes, **Alton Priors** N.W. of Pewsey
825 Aweltun 1086 Aultone, Awltone, Auuiltone 1155 Awelton 1199 Aulton Prioris 1268 Awelton Berners 1320 Aulton Berner 1512 Aulton Barones

From OE *æwielle-tun*, 'farmstead by the well or river source', after a tributary of the Salisbury Avon which rises in a low-lying meadow between the two villages. *Berners* is a post-Conquest family name (a Fine of 1320 mentions John and Adam Berner), and Alton Barnes was once part of the same estate as nearby STANTON ST BERNARD, which takes its name from the same family. Alton Priors formerly belonged to the monastery of St Swithun at Winchester. Of the early forms above, *Aultone* and *Awltone* refer to Alton Priors.

Alvediston (alston, aston) S. of Tisbury
1166 de Alfwieteston Abbtisse, Alvitheston c1190 Alvideston 1214 Alvitheston 1287 Albedeston 1428 Alveston 1571 Alstone

Probably 'Ælfgeat's tun or farmstead'. *Aileva*, a descendant of the original tenant, is recorded as holding two hides of land here at the time of Edward the Confessor. The village was part of the Chalk estate, granted to the abbey at Wilton in 955.

Amesbury
858 Amberesburg 880 Ambresbyrig 932 Ambresburch 972 Hambresburuh 1086 Amblesberie, Ambresberie 1227 Amesbury, Ambresburi 1231 Aumbresberia 1265 Ambrebiry 1289 Estambrebur' 1322 Great Aumbresburi 1332 Ambresburi Priorisse 1335 Ambresburye Magna 1434 Almesberie

A fine array of names for this centre of ancient Wessex, which takes its name from the Iron Age hillfort (popularly known as Vespasian's Camp, after the Roman conqueror) on a spur to the west of the town. Amesbury has traditionally been connected with Aurelius Ambrosius, who founded his fortress capital here in the 5th century. A contemporary of the enigmatic King Arthur, Ambrosius was made King of the Romano-British in 464 and struggled against the invading Saxons for almost fifty years. Hence the name is *Ambre's burh*, meaning 'the fortified place of Ambrosius'. An abbey was founded here c979 and this was replaced by a new priory in 1177. The Welsh knew Amesbury as *Caer Emrys*, while locally it was also known as *Ambresbury* until the 19th century.

Ansty S. of Tisbury
1086 Anestige 1220 Anesty 1245 Ansteia 1316 Anestigh

Situated at the foot of Ansty Coombe, the village probably derives its name from OE *anstig*, denoting a narrow path or passage up a steep hill. Longstaff interprets the name as 'Ansger's stile'.

Ashley N.W. of Bradford
1279 Ashelegh 1332 Aysshelegh 1492 Aissheley

OE *æsch-leah*, 'ash-tree meadow or clearing'.

Ashton Gifford or **Giffard** S.E. of Warminster
1242 Aston 1247 Ayston 1279 Eston Giffard 1281 Aihston 1327 Asshetone 1357 Ashtone Giffard

Originally OE *æscan-tun*, 'ash-tree farmstead'. Elias *Giffard*, whose ancestors probably came from the village of Giffard near Rouen in Normandy, held the manor in 1242. See ELSTON.

Ashton Keynes W. of Cricklade
880/5 Æsctun 1086 Essitone 1281 Eshton 1306 Asshton next Crykelade 1386 Asheton by Cheleworth 1428 Assheton 1572 Aysheton Keynes

'Ash-tree farmstead', as ASHTON GIFFORD. *Keynes* was the name of former Lords of the Manor. William de Keynes held the estate in 1256. The family originated from the village of Cahagnes in Normandy.

Ashton, West S.E. of Trowbridge
1248 in Westaston 1279 Gyldeneaston 1485 Gyldon Ashton 1485 West Aissheton

See ASHTON GIFFORD. West Ashton, with neighbouring ROOD ASHTON and STEEPLE ASHTON, was part of the former Ashton estate. *Gylden* is probably descriptive of a wealthy manor ('golden') and refers specifically to East Town Farm.

Atworth N.W. of Melksham
1001 at Attenwrthe 1249 de Attewurthe 1402 Atteworth Cotell 1404 Little Cotels, Cotels Atteward 1427 Ateford 1428 Parva Atteworth 1451 Mechell Attewarde 1458 Great Atte Ward 1489 Atward

'Ætta's worth or homestead: *Atteworth Cotell*, also known as Little Atworth, and now called Cottles, takes its name from the French family: it was held by Richard *Cotel* in 1242. *Mechell* or *michel* (from OE *michel*) are synonyms for 'Great', used to distinguish the larger settlement. Locally known as Atford.

Avebury (abury)
1086 de Aureberie 1114 Avesbiria 1189 Aveberia 1227 Avebure 1256 Avesbyry 1268 Avenebyr' 1279 Avebere Priur 1494 Aubury

The second element was once thought to be OE *burh* or *byrig*, 'fortified place'. However, although Avebury is the largest henge monument in Britain, dating from 3000–2000BC, there is general agreement that it was of ritual rather than defensive significance. The 17th century antiquarian John Aubrey mistakenly took the name to mean 'old bury'. More likely, as the earlier forms suggest, is OE *berie* or *beria*, 'open field', which well describes

The Entrance of Kennet avenue into Abury 14. May 1724.

the rolling chalk downland around the village. The derivation of the first element is uncertain, but suggestions include the personal name *Afa* or the river name Avon (possibly a forgotten Celtic name for the local Winterbourne). The early references show confusion between the letters 'u' and 'v', which in DB were indistinguishable from each other. There was a small priory here in the Middle Ages.

Avon N.E. of Chippenham
688 (juxta flumen) Avene, Abon, Avon 940 be Afene 1065 Auene (terra) 1194 de Auene 1262 of Havene

Avon comes from an ancient Celtic substantival word which was widely used as a generic term for streams and rivers. As the 940 form shows, the precise meaning of the place-name is 'settlement by the (Bristol) Avon'. The earlier Saxon references apply to the river rather than the settlement on its banks.

Avoncliff (aincliff, ankley) S.W. of Bradford
Hen. II Aveneclife 1249 Aveneclive 1432 Aveneclyfessmille 1554 Anclyff

Named from the steep northern face of the river-cliff which overlooks the village and the River Avon.

Axford E. of Marlborough
1184 in Axeford 1217 Axeford 1289 Assheford

There was a ford here across the River Kennet, probably on Stone Lane, leading to Savernake Forest: the river crossing is marked by a sarsen stone set into the southern bank of the river. The first element is either the personal name *Aska* or OE *æsca*, 'ash-tree'. Hence 'Aska's ford' or 'ford by the ash'.

Badbury S.E. of Swindon
955 Baddeburi, de Baddeborwe 1086 Badeberie 1249 Baddebyr 1428 Badebury

'Badda's *burh* or fortified place', a reference to the Iron Age hillfort on nearby LIDDINGTON Hill, which was known in the past as Badbury Hill. The presence of the name *Badda* has led many historians to believe that Badbury Hill was *Mons Badonicus*, the fabled site of King Arthur's victory over the Saxon forces c500. Other authorities place the battle at BAYDON.

Bapton W. of Wylye
1221 Babinton 1276 Babeton 1312 Babyngton 1413 Babbeton

OE *Babban-tun*, 'Babba's farmstead', possibly a reference to the person who also founded BAVERSTOCK, six miles distant.

Barbury Castle S. of Swindon
556 æt Beran byrig 1180 Bereberia 1252 Berebyrie 1428 Berbury

'Bera's hillfort'. Barbury Castle is an Iron Age earthwork dating from the

2nd century BC. The 556 reference is taken from the Anglo-Saxon Chronicle, which records that "In this year Cynric and Caewlin fought against the Britons *æt Beran byrig*".

Barford Park N. of Downton
1086 Bereford

See BARFORD, below. Creation of the medieval park involved the destruction of the original village of Barford.

Barford St Martin W. of Wilton
1086 Bereford 1304 Berevord St Martin 1335 Bereford St Martin's 1461 Bereforth

Possibly includes the same first element as in BARBURY, giving 'Bera's ford'. A more likely interpretation is OE *bere-ford*, 'ford by the barley-field' or 'ford across which barley is carried'. The ford probably lay at the end of Green Lane, which leads southwards past the 13th century church of St Martin to the River Nadder.

Bathampton (battington) E. of Wylye
1086 Bachentune 1194 de Bathaton 1222 Bethampton 1242 Bachamwyly 1258 Bathamwyly 1279 Bathampton 1382 Batamtounewyly 1428 Badampton

OE *bath-ham-tun* is 'farmstead by the bathing-place'. The original name of this estate on the Wylye was possibly plain Hampton.

Baverstock W. of Wilton
968 æt Babanstoce, Babbanstoc 1086 Babestoche 1225 in Babestok, Babbestoch' 1428 Babestok 1535 Baberstoke 1568 Baverstoke

From *Babban-stoc*, meaning 'Babba's settlement'. The OE word *stoc* has several interpretations, but is widely believed to derive from a stake, or an enclosure fenced in by stocks or posts to form a settlement. See also BAPTON.

Baydon N. of Ramsbury
1146 Beidona 1226 Beidon 1241 Bedon 1294 Beydon 1399 Beydoun

It has been suggested that the first element is a personal name, *Beaza*. Ekwall prefers OE *beg-dun*, 'berry down', or possibly *beo-dun*, 'bee down'. The forms are too late to ascertain whether Baydon is in fact *Mons Badonicus*, site of the legendary 6th century battle but, on the whole, *Badbury* seems a more probable location.

Baynton N.E. of Westbury
1203 de Beinton 1204 Bainton 1208 Beynton 1330 Benton 1348 Beyntonesfeld

'Bæga's or Bæda's farmstead'. Or possibly the first element is similar to that in BAYDON.

Beanacre (binager) N. of Melksham
1261 Benacr' 1276 Benacre Edw.I Benakere 1573 Beneger al. Benacre

From OE *bean-æcer*, 'bean-field'.

Beckhampton (beckington) S.W. of Avebury
1086 Bachentune 1242 de Bachampton 1249 Bechampton 1268 Bakanton 13th c. Bakhamtun 1316 Bakhampton 1493 Bakehampton

The DB entry would suggest that the meaning is *Baccan-tun*, 'Bacca's or Bucca's farmstead': see BEECHINGSTOKE. However, the later forms spell the second element clearly as *-hampton* ('homestead'). Another explanation, which I favour, is OE *bæc-hean-tun*, meaning 'settlement by the high back or ridge', possibly referring to the marked ridge between the Winterbourne stream and Beckhampton village.

Bedwyn, Great and **Little** S.E. of Marlborough
778 Bedewinde, in bedewindan c880 æt Bedewindan c1016 Bedeuuinde 1086 Bedvinde, Bedvine 1091 Bedewinde 1177 Estbedewinda 1199 Bedewyna 1276 Chepingbedewynde 1310 Estbedewynde 1441 Westbedwynd 1484 Bedewen 1502 Bedwyn Abbotes 1547 Grete-, Lyttelbedwyn

Possibly the name comes from the Wiltshire dialect word *bedwine* or *bedwind*, a term used to describe the wild clematis plant which is a native of the county. Alternatively, it may derive from a Celtic stream-name of obscure meaning: *bedewindan* in the Saxon charter dated 778 evidently refers to the small tributary of the Kennet which runs here. East and West Bedwyn were Little and Great Bedwyn respectively. Formerly a borough of some importance, Great Bedwyn had its own mint, and was the chief settlement in the Royal Forest of Savernake. As the 1276 reference suggests, Great Bedwyn was the site of a weekly market (OE *ceap*). In 1443, its High Street was known as *Chepyngstrete*, also from the market. Bedwyn was eclipsed in importance by Marlborough during the Middle Ages.

Beechingstoke E. of Devizes
941 Stoke 1086 Bichenstoch 13th c. Stokes in Kanyngemershe 1428 in Bychenstoke 1431 Bychyngstoke 1513 Bechynstoke

OE *stoc*, 'settlement', was the original Saxon place-name: see BAVERSTOCK. The first element is a personal name, *Bucca* or *Bicca*, the latter being a derisory nickname from OE *bicca* ('bitch'). Situated on the south-east edge of the former Cannings Marsh (see ALL CANNINGS). Known locally as Stoke until the 19th century, and also spelled Beachingstoke on some maps.

Bemerton W. of Salisbury
1086 Bimertone 1107 Beomertone 1249 Bymerton 1259 Bimberton 1281 Bumerton 1290 Bym̃tone 1306 Bymirtone 1316 Bymerton 1426 Bemerton

An Anglo-Saxon charter records *to bymera cumbe* in the vicinity. Either OE *bymera-tun*, 'farmstead of the trumpeters', or *Beornmoer-tun*, denoting the home of a Saxon lord.

Bentley Wood E. of Salisbury
1178 Bentleswuda *1227 Bentlewud* *1270 Bentelleswod*

Originally OE *beonet-leah*, meaning 'bent clearing' or 'clearing where the bent-grass grows'.

Berwick Bassett (barrik, berrik) N. of Avebury
1168 Berwicha *1206 Berewyc* *1321 Berewykbasset* *1325 Berwyk Basset* *1449 Barwyk Basset*

OE *berewic* means 'the grange, or outlying part of the estate, where the barley grows' or possibly 'the shed in which barley is stored'. Wick is a common suffix and may also be interpreted as 'dwelling, hamlet or dairy-farm'. Alan *Basset* held the manor in 1211; his family name is a post-Conquest one which also recurs in COMPTON BASSETT, EASTON BASSETT, WINTERBOURNE BASSETT and WOOTTON BASSETT.

Berwick St James E. of Wylye
1086 Wintreburne *c1190 Berewyk Sancti Jacobi* *1275 Bewike* *1324 Beriwyk*

See BERWICK BASSETT. The Norman church is dedicated to St James. The DB entry refers to the old name for the River Till, so-called because it is reduced to a streamlet during the summer months. Other Wiltshire villages described as *Wintreburne* in DB but now known by other names are ELSTON, MDDINGTON, RABSON, ROLLESTON and SHREWTON — all except Rabson are upstream from Berwick St James on the Till.

Berwick St John E. of Shaftesbury
1167 Berwicha *1196 Berewic* *1265 de Berewyke S. Johannis* *1316 de Berewyke* *1536 Barwyke Seynt John*

See BERWICK BASSETT. The 13th century church is dedicated to St John.

Berwick St Leonard E. of Hindon
Hen.I Berewica *1291 Berwyk Sci Leonardi* *1545 Barwyke alias Cold Barwyke*

See BERWICK BASSETT. The church is dedicated to St Leonard. Cold Berwick Hill still exists in the parish.

Beversbrook N.E. of Calne
1086 Bevresbroc, Brevresbrok *c1240 Beverbrok* *1428 Beveresbroke*

OE *befor-broc*, 'beaver's brook', with reference to a tributary of the Marden now called Fisher's Brook. The beaver has been extinct in England since about the 13th century. A Saxon charter at nearby Kington St Michael mentions a stream called *beuerbourne*. The road to the farm is called Beaversbrook Lane.

Biddestone W. of Chippenham
1086 Bedestone *1187 Bedenseton'* *1215 in Buddeston'* *1285 Budisdene*

1297 Biedestone 1321 Butteston 1339 Byddeston 1428 Butteston 1539 Bittson

Probably 'Byda's or Bieda's farmstead'.

Bincknoll (bynal) S.E. of Wootton Bassett
1086 in Bechenhalle c1220 Bienknoll 1247 de Benknolle 1268 Bencholl 1367 Bikenolle 1429 Byngknoll

Either OE *beona-cnoll*, 'bee's mound or summit', although more likely is *Biccan-heall*, 'Bicca's palace or residence', incorporating the same personal name as BEECHINGSTOKE. There was a Norman castle here, so it is possible that the name could refer to some earlier structure on this prominent site atop the Lower Chalk escarpment. The 13th century versions show Norman influence, and confusion with the French 'bien' in the first element.

Bishop's Cannings N.E. of Devizes
1086 Cainingham 1091 Caninges 1226 Kaning 1294 Canyng Episcopi 1296 Canygges Bishop's 1314 Bisshopescanyngges 1491 Bishops Canynges

The DB reference shows that this village was once the *ham* or hamlet attached to ALL CANNINGS. The Bishop of Sarum was chief tenant here in the 11th century.

Bishopstone (bushton) E. of Swindon
1186 Bissopeston 1249 Byssupeston' 1300 Bysshopeston 1534 Bussheton

From OE *biscopes-tun*, 'bishop's farmstead or estate'. Bishopstone was formerly an outlying part of the parish of Ramsbury, which belonged to the Bishop of Salisbury.

Bishopstone S. of Wilton
1166 Bissopeston 1244 Ebleburn Bissopiston 1249 Byssupeston 1268 Byscopeston 1310 Ebbelesbourne Episcopi 1428 Bysshopeston 1534 Bussheton

See BISHOPSTONE, above. Formerly the property of the Bishop of Winchester. The older name of Ebbesbourne Bishops was used to distinguish the village from EBBESBOURNE WAKE, from which estate it was formed. Bishopstone became the accepted name during the later Middle Ages. Compare the current form of this name with BUSHTON, which has a similar derivation.

Bishopstrow S.E. of Warminster
1086 Biscopestreu 1196 Bisuppestru 1236 Bisshopestre 1270 Byscoppestrewe Edw.I Bissupestreo 1365 Busshepestrowe

Originally *biscopes-treow*, 'bishop's cross or tree'. Jones says that the name refers to a cross which once stood here as a memorial to St Aldhelm, abbot of Malmesbury and Bishop of Sherborne, to whom the village church is dedicated. According to another legend told by William of Malmesbury, St

BISHOP CANNINGS CHURCH, WILTSHIRE.

Aldhelm once preached at *Biscepes truue* and, on placing his ashen staff into the earth, it multiplied into a wood of ash-trees.

Blackland S.E. of Calne
1195 Blakeland c1290 de Blockelonde 1428 Blackelond

Possibly named after the colour of the soil, although it could well refer to a tract of land covered by dark forest, in this case part of the ancient BLACKMORE Forest linking PEWSHAM and SELWOOD Forests.

Blackmore N.E. of Melksham
1338 de Blakhemore 1230 Blakemore

OE *mor* meant 'a tract of waste ground or marsh', with reference here to the 'waste' land covered by Blackmore Forest. Blackmore was largely disafforested during the 17th century.

Blunsdon, Broad and **Blunsdon St Andrew** N. of Swindon
1086 Blontesdone, Bluntesdone 1242 Churibluntesdon 1263 Brodebluntesdon 1277 Hangindebluntesdon 1281 Bluntesdon Seynt Andreu 1316 de Bluntesdone Sancti Leonardi, Bluntesdone Sancti Andree 1348 Blountesdon Gay 1397 Lytelblountesdon 1544 Androblunsdon 1650 Blountesdon

The name Blunsdon means 'Blunt's hill' (OE *dun*) and refers to an early Lord of the Manor whose name appears in the Battle Abbey Roll. *Churi* is derived from OE *cirice* ('church') and describes the church at Broad Blunsdon, which is dedicated to St Leonard. *Broad* is derived from an OE word meaning 'great' and denotes the larger of the two settlements. Broad Blunsdon was also known as Blunsdon Gay (after Walter *le Gay*, who owned part of the manor in 1281) and Hanging Blunsdon, with reference to its position on the steep north-facing scarp: two farms are now called The Hangings. St Andrew is the dedication of the 13th century church at Blunsdon St Andrew, which was also known as Little Blunsdon. See also BURY BLUNSDON.

Boscombe S.E. of Amesbury
1086 Boscumbe 1199 in Boscumbe 1256 Borrescumb' 1270 Bescumba c1290 Bozscumbe 1364 Borescombe 1428 Boscombe

Probably derived from *Boran-cumb*, 'Bora's combe or small valley'. The village is on the River Bourne. *Bors* is an OE word meaning 'something spiky or prickly'.

Bottlesford W. of Pewsey
892 to botan waelle 933 to botan wylle 1348 Bottewelleford

The original form means 'Bota's well, spring or stream', the personal name here being a familiar form of *Botwine* or *Beowulf*. 'Ford' is a later addition and refers to the crossing-point of the stream which forms the western boundary of Manningford parish.

Bowden Hill and **Bowden Park** S.W. of Calne
c1240 Bovedon 1374 Bouedon

OE *Bofan-dun*, 'Bofa's hill', or *bufan-dun*, 'place above the hill'. Nearby BOWOOD shares the same first element.

Bowerchalke (Bower Chalke) (burchalk) S.W. of Broad Chalke
826 to cealcan gemere 955 æt Ceolcum 974 Cheolca 1086 Chelche 1237 Shalke 1242 Chalke 1268 de Burchalke 1276 Boure Chalke 1279 Burghchalke 1482 Bery Chalke 1553 West Chauke

From an ancient Saxon simplex form, *cealc*, meaning 'place of chalk' or 'the chalk downs': the village lies in the White Chalk district. There is a hillfort on nearby Marleycombe Hill, so 'Bower' is possibly a corruption of ME *burh* (see BURTON), particularly in view of the current pronounciation. Or the name may come from *bower corn*, an old expression for grain rents. The references prior to 1268 include the neighbouring village of BROAD CHALKE. The 955 form appears in a grant of land from King Eadwic to the nuns of Wilton, and also encompasses the villages of ALVEDISTON, BERWICK ST JOHN and SEMLEY.

Bowood S.W. of Calne
13th c. Bowoda Hen.III Bunewode 1319 Bouewode

OE *Bofan-wudu*, 'Bofa's wood', or *bufan-wudu*, 'place above the wood', both referring to its position by SELWOOD Forest. See also BOWDEN.

Box N. of Bradford
1144 Boczam 1181 La Boxe 1216 la Bosse 1249 in Boxle 1316 de Boxe 1435 Box

Simply from the OE *box*, which can be interpreted as 'place where the box-trees grow'. Writing in 1685, John Aubrey observed that the box trees were 'now worne out'. *Boczam* was probably pronounced 'Boxham' and *Boxle* 'Boxley'.

Boyton S.E. of Heytesbury
1086 Boientone 1252 Boyton 1366 Boynton

From an original *Boian-tun*, 'Boia's farmstead'. The personal name is of Celtic origin.

Bradenstoke-cum-Clack (braidstoke) S.W. of Wootton Bassett
1086 Bradenstoche, Stoche 1244 Bradenstok 1290 Bradestok 1310 Clak' 1342 Clacke

The pre-Conquest name was probably Stoke, from OE *stoc*, meaning 'settlement' (see BAVERSTOCK). Bradenstoke thus indicates a settlement built in a clearing of the ancient BRADON Forest. The ruins of Bradenstoke Abbey, a former Augustinian priory, stand near the village — Burton Bradstock in Dorset takes part of its name from the priory, which once held lands there. Clack was an alternative name for the village until the 19th century and derives from Clack Mount, an earthwork on the scarp edge to the north-east of Bradenstoke Farm (*klack* is the Swedish word for a knoll or

Bradenstoke Priory

small hill). Once locally known as Lousy Clack, from OE *hlaw*, 'funeral mound', an element which also occurs in CHEDGLOW and WINTERSLOW.

Bradford-on-Avon
652 æt Bradanforda be afne 705 Bradanford 1001 æt Bradeforda 1086 Bradeford 1340 Brodeford 1415 Bradford

This important town on the Bristol Avon has appeared in many written records over the years, and its name remains remarkably true to its original form, OE *bradan-ford*, which describes the river crossing on a broad bend of the Avon. Alternatively, the first element may be a personal name, *Brada*. The 652 reference comes from the Anglo-Saxon Chronicle, which records a battle waged here by King Cenwalh of Wessex. See also AVON.

Bradley, North S. of Trowbridge
1174 Bradlega c1291 de Bradeleye 1316 Bradele 1352 North Bradlegh 1632 North Broadly

From OE *bradan-leah*, 'wide clearing or meadow'. 'North' in relation to nearby MAIDEN BRADLEY, or because of its position on the former northern edge of Selwood Forest.

Bratton Church, 1860

Bratton E. of Westbury
1177 Bratton 1196 Bractone 1221 Bracton 1267 Bretton 1316 de Brattone

Brada-tun, 'the broad enclosure', or possibly *bræc-tun*, 'farmstead by the newly-cultivated land'. The stream which runs northwards to Semington Brook is sometimes locally called the Bratt, but this is probably a back-formation from the original village name, ie. the stream took its name from the village and not vice-versa.

Braydon or **Bradon** E. of Malmesbury
688 Silva Bradon 796 silva Braden 901 Bradene c925 on Bradene 1065 Bradon 1243 Bradon 1311 Braddene

The name Bradon was formerly applied to the great swath of forest (Latin *silva*) that covered the whole of north Wiltshire, reaching south to Bradford-on-Avon and eastwards to the Vale of the White Horse. In 1222 Bradon Forest ranked second in all England for the number of timber trees it contained, but it was largely disafforested during the reign of King Charles II. PEWSHAM and BLACKMORE Forests were extensions of Bradon. The present parish of Braydon originated from an early land-clearance in the central part of the forest. The name is possibly OE *braden-denu*, 'wide valley', although the earliest version, from an Anglo-Saxon charter, clearly records the second element as *don* ('hill'). A more likely explanation is the word *den*, a term used to describe a wooded valley or woodland suited to pasturage: many forests were formerly regulated by Courts of Dens. Braydon Pond was known as *Wulfmere* in Saxon days. Writing in 1540, Leland comments that "al the quarters of the foreste of Braden be welle woodid even along from Malmesbyri to Chippenham". The scattered settlement of the Leigh-Minety-Brinkworth area is indicative of piecemeal forest clearance over the centuries. See also BRADENSTOKE.

Bremhill (brimble) E. of Chippenham
937 Broemel, Bremel 1065 Bremela 1086 Breme 1196 Bremleia, Bromel 1226 Bremleshill 1268 Brembel 1316 Bromell 1540 Bremyll

Derived from OE *bremel* meaning, in this instance, 'place where bramble grows'. The suffix 'hill' is a later development, being a corruption of the original second syllable.

Bremilham S.W. of Malmesbury
1065 Bremelham 1178 Brumilham 1270 Brimelham 1404 Bremulham

OE *bremel-ham*, 'homestead by the bramble or broom'. Or possibly the ending is *-hamm*, a word used to describe a meadow enclosed by water: the hamlet is situated in a wide bend of the Bristol Avon. Also known as Cowage (*1256 Cuwike; 1275 Cowiche; c1290 Cowyk*), meaning 'outlying cow-farm' (OE *cu-wic*). Bremilham is an unsignposted settlement near FOXHAM.

Brigmerston N. of Amesbury
1086 Brismartone 1204 in Brictmareston 1270 Briggesmareston

1273Bryhtmerston   1316 Brightmershton   1412 Brikmerston

OE *Beorhtmoeres-tun*, 'the farmstead of Beorhtmoer'. *Brismar*, probably a descendant of the original owner, was a landholder here at the time of Edward the Confessor.

Brinkworth N.W. of Wootton Bassett
1065 Brinkwrtha   1086 Brenchewrde, Brecheorde   1190 Brinkeswurda   1191 Brinkeworth   1194 de Brincewrthe   1236 Brenkewurth   1428 Brunkeworth

Literally 'the farmstead on the brink of a hill' (OE *brinc-weorth*), ie. the Callow Hill ridge. Another example of a hilltop 'worth' is provided by HIGHWORTH. Alternatively, the first element may be *Brynca*, a recorded personal name.

Britford (burford) S.E. of Salisbury
670 to Bryt. ford, Brytfordingea landscære   826 to bridforda, Brutford   997 to Brytford   1065 æt Brytfordan   1086 Bretford, Bredford   c1100 Brytford   1203 Brideford   1227 Bratford   1273 Brutford   1488 Birtford

From an original OE *Bryttan-ford*, 'ford of the Britons', possibly in memory of some historic occasion when the British captured a strategic crossing-point on the Salisbury Avon from the Saxon invaders. *Landscære* in the 670 charter refers to the boundary with BISHOPSTONE. Burford is a modern corruption of the 15th century form.

Brixton Deverill S. of Warminster
1086 Devrel   1229 Britricheston   1242 Brightricheston   1316 Brighteston   1410 Brighston Deverell

Probably derived from OE *Beorhtrices-tun* ('Beorhtric's farm'): a descendant of the original owner, named *Brihtric*, was tenant here during the reign of Edward the Confessor. A reference to *Ecgbryhtesstan* in the Anglo-Saxon Chronicle may refer to Brixton Deverill: *Ecgbryhtesstan* is described as standing 'to the east of SELWOOD' and is the place where King Alfred met his forces in 878 before the Battle of EDINGTON. The name Deverill has been the subject of much conjecture — it possibly comes from *dubro*, a Celtic stream-name meaning 'water', with a diminutive suffix *-ial*, ie. 'little stream'; Hoare suggests *dive-rill*, 'stream that dives' because the river Wylye flows underground until surfacing at Kingston Deverill, upstream; a more fanciful suggestion is that Deverill is a corrupted form of *D'Evereux*, former Earls of Salisbury. The 1086 DB entry applies to the area around the Wylye headwaters, and also includes HILL DEVERILL, KINGSTON DEVERILL, LONGBRIDGE DEVERILL and MONKTON DEVERILL. The river is recorded as *DeFereal* in a charter of King Edgar dated 968.

Broad Blunsdon

See BLUNSDON, BROAD.

Broad Chalke (Broad Chalk) S.W. of Wilton
1289 Magna Chelk   1312 Grete Chalke   1316 de Chalke   1380 Brode

Chalk *1415 Brodechalke* *1553 Est Chauke*

The prefixes all refer to this village's size and position in relation to nearby Bower Chalke. For forms prior to 1289, see BOWER CHALKE. *Broad* is an archaic term for 'Great'.

Broad Hinton S.E. of Wootton Bassett
1086 Hantone, Hentone *1232 Henton* *1319 Brodehenton* *1428 Henton Columbers, Henton Waas*

Originally OE *hean-tun*, 'high town', descriptive of the village's position on top of the Lower Chalk escarpment. 'Broad' in relation to HINTON PARVA. Matthew *de Columbariis* had a holding here in the 13th century, likewise John *Waas* two centuries later.

Broad Town S.E. of Wootton Bassett
1205 Labradeton *1206 Bradetone* *1220 de la Bradetune* *1280 Brodetoun* *1322 Broddeton*

Identical in derivation to BRATTON (*brada-tun*). This is 'the great farmstead', in relation to the smaller estate of Little Town nearby. The 1205 form includes the French article, *la*.

Brokenborough N.W. of Malmesbury
956 Brokenberga, brokene beregge *1065 Brokenberg* *1086 Brocheneberge* *1235 in Brokeberwe* *1340 Brokenbergh* *1394 Brokynborgh* *1428 Brokynborgh*

OE *broken-beorg*, 'crumbling or broken hill or barrow'. According to Jones, an old settlement on the Bristol Avon here was *Caerdurburg*, 'the ancient fort of the Saxon kings'. The present name possibly originates from when the fort was overthrown and destroyed.

Bromham N.W. of Devizes
1086 Bromham, Brumham *1168 Bramham*

OE *brom-ham* or *-hamm*, 'homestead or enclosure where the broom grows'.

Broughton Gifford N.E. of Bradford
1001 Broctun *1007 at Broctune* *1086 Broctone* *1267 Brochetone* *1279 Brouhton* *1278 Broctun Magna* *1288 Broctun Giffard* *1409 Braghton Gyffard*

Broughton is a common English place-name, and comes from OE *broc-tun*, 'farmstead on the brook', in this case an affluent of the Bristol Avon. John, 1st Baron *Giffard*, held the manor during Richard I's reign, and Gifford Hall perpetuates the family name: see also ASHTON GIFFORD, ELSTON and FONTHILL GIFFORD. Named *Broctun Magna* to distinguish from the smaller village of *Broctun Parva*, now known as MONKTON FARLEIGH.

Bugley W. of Warminster
1236 Buggele *1256 in Buggel̄* *Edw.I in Bugelighe* *1332 Bogelegh* *1350 Boggeleye* *1351 Bogley* *1536 Buggeley*

Probably from *Buggan-leah*, 'Bugga's clearing or meadow'. *Bugge* was the daughter of King Centwine. Alternatively, the first element may be ME *bugge*, 'hobgoblin'.

Bulbridge S.W. of Wilton
c1200 de Bolebrigge, de Bulebrige 1275 Bollebrugge c1290 Bolebrygg

OE *bulan-brycg*, 'bull-bridge', marking a crossing-point over the River Nadder on the old road from Wilton towards Hampshire. That a bridge existed here as early as 1200 is indicative of Bulbridge's former importance on this route.

Bulford N.E. of Amesbury
1178 Bultisford 1249 Bultingford 1270 Bultesford 1316 de Bollforde 1341 Bultford 1428 Bolteford 1566 Bulford

Although the first element is today identical to that in BULBRIDGE, the early forms are sufficiently different to assume an original OE *Bultan-ford*, 'Bulta's ford'. Bulford lies at the confluence of the Avon and Nine Mile River.

Bulkington S.W. of Devizes
1086 Boltintone 1211 Bolkintone 1225 in Bulkinton' 1324 Bulkynton 1437 Bulkyndoun

OE *Bulcan-tun*, 'Bulca's farmstead'.

Bupton S.W. of Wootton Bassett
1232 in Bubbeclive 1336 Bobbeton 1488 Bubton

The original name would seem to be OE *Bubban-clif*, 'Bubba's cliff', particularly as this settlement is so near to CLYFFE PYPARD on the steep Lower Chalk escarpment. In 1232 William Quintin gave to Bradenstoke Abbey five acres of land *in Bubbeclive*. William Bubbe *owed service in Clyve* in 1255. The present name is a late *tun*-formation, ie. of post-Saxon origin.

Burbage S.E. of Marlborough
961 Burhbece' c1000 Burhbec 1086 Burbetce, Buberge 1139 Burbecha 1158 Burbeche 1177 Burbache 1194 Burggebge 1229 Borebache 1321 Burbachesauvage

The first element seems to be OE *burh*, 'earthwork or town'. The second is less obvious, and could be either *bece*, 'beech-tree or beech-wood', or *bæc*, 'ridge'. Part of the parish belonged to the Savage family before passing to the Longspées during the reign of Henry III.

Burcombe W. of Wilton
937 Brydancumb 1086 Bredecumbe 1225 Brudecumba 1268 Bridecumbe Salvage 1282 Northbrudekumbe 1302 Bridecumbe 1345 Southbrudecombe 1481 Northbritcombe 1540 Burdcombe 1572 Boorecombe

OE *Brydan-cumb*, 'Bryda's combe or small valley', probably referring to the dry valley south of the village. See BRIDMORE. Owned by the Savage family in the 13th century: see also BURBAGE.

Burton E. of Mere
1204 Burinton' 1236 Burtona 1268 Burghton 1314 Mereburton 1327 Bourton

From OE *burh-tun*, 'farm by the earthwork or enclosed settlement', ie. the town of Mere.

Bury Blunsdon N. of Swindon
1279 Buriblunesdon c1300 Buriblunsdon 1319 Burbluntesdon

See BLUNSDON. The prefix is OE *burh* or *byrig*, 'fortified place', referring to the Iron Age camp on Castle Hill. Now more commonly known as Burytown.

Bushton S. of Wootton Bassett
1242 Bissopeston 1316 Bishoppeston

See BISHOPSTONE. Held in the 11th century by the Bishop of Winchester. The original name has since been shortened by the vagaries of local dialect.

Buttermere S. of Hungerford
863 Butermere 931 æt Buter mere Will.I Bwtoermærae 1086 Butremare 12th c. Buttermere 1276 Botermere 1373 Boturmere

Presumably this is OE *butere-mere*, literally 'pool with butter-coloured water'. However, the absence of any expanse of water nearby and the village's proximity to the border with Hampshire makes the alternative *Buteran-mære*, 'Buter's boundary or landmark', seem more credible.

Cadenham N. of Calne
1086 Cadeham 1242 Kadenham 1468 Cadenham 1595 Cadnam

The *ham* or homestead of *Cada*, possibly the same man who gave his name to nearby Catcombe (*1114 Cadecoma; 1241 in Cadecumb*) and Cat Brook. Or the first element may be the Latin *coed*, *caid*, 'wood'.

Calcutt S.E. of Cricklade
1086 Colecote 1404 Calcote 1493 in Calecote 1773 Corkett

Probably *Colan-cote*, 'the cottages belonging to Cola'.

Calne (caan)
955 Calne 997 Calnæ 1086 Cauna 1091 Calna 1160 Canna 1236 Kaune 1556 Cawne

This name has Celtic (or possibly pre-Celtic) roots and is identical in derivation to Colne in Lancashire, *col-aun*, meaning 'current of waters'. Colne is a frequently-encountered British stream-name, and Calne probably took its name from the small river, now called Marden Brook, on which it stands. See also CALSTONE WELLINGTON. The 955 reference comes from the will of the West Saxon king, Eadred; the 997 form appears in the Anglo-Saxon Chronicle in connection with a visit to the town by King Ethelred.

The Arms of the Borough of Calne

Calstone Wellington (wilıngton) S.E. of Calne
1086 Calestone 1130 Calestona 1164 Calestoñ 1242 Calston 1500 Calston Wely 1568 Caulston Wellington

Calstone is composed of the Scandinavian personal name *Kale* and OE *tun*, forming 'Kale's farmstead'. Or possibly the first element is related to the name of nearby CALNE. Lord Ralph Willington, otherwise Ralph *de Wylyton*, the owner of Devizes Castle, held the village in 1254.

Castle Combe N.W. of Chippenham
1086 Come 1186 Cumbe 1270 Castelcumbe 1305 Chastelcombe 1315 Castelcombe 1422 Castelcome

The village is situated in the winding valley formed by the By Brook, whence it derives its name, OE *cumb*. The castle which once stood to the north of Castle Combe was destroyed by the Danes in 878. A Norman castle was built on the site by Walter de Dunstanvilles in the reign of King Stephen, but this too was in ruins by the time of Henry IV.

Castle Eaton N.E. of Cricklade
1086 Ettone 1218 Etun c1290 Eaton Meysy 1442 Easte Yetton 1469 Castell Eton c1540 Eiton Castelle

Situated near the Thames, the name means 'enclosure by water' (*ea-tun*), but there are no records of a castle ever standing here. The manor was owned by the *Meysi* family, who also held nearby MARSTON MEYSEY, during the 13th century. *Easte Yetton* is to distinguish from WATER EATON.

Chaddenwick (Charnage) E. of Mere
1086 Chedelwich 1196 Chadelewic 1224 Chadenwik 1294 Chadewiz 1332 Chadewyche 1822 Chadenwych sometimes called Charnage

Probably from OE *Ceadelan-wic*, 'Ceadela's dairy-farm or grange'. Charnage is a late corruption of the original name.

Chalfield, Great and **Little** (chavill) N.E. of Bradford
1001 Chaldfeld 1086 Caldefelle 1196 Chaudefeld 1199 Chadesfeld, Kaldefeld 1201 Scaudefeld 1281 Cheldefeld 1428 Est, West Chaldefeld 1526 Chaldevile 1659 Little Chavill

The villages are on an exposed, north-facing slope, and the name derives from OE *cealda-feld*, 'bleak or windswept open field or common land'. Great and Little Chalfield were *Est* and *West Chaldefeld* respectively.

Chapmanslade S.W. of Westbury
1245 Chipmannesled 1268 Chypmaneslad 1455 Chipmanslade

Although there are no forms earlier than the 13th century to go by, the name appears to be OE *ceapmannes-lade*, 'the roadway of, or frequented by, the chapmen or merchants'. *Ceap* is the same element found in *chepyng*, 'market' — see BEDWYN. Chapmanslade is situated on the Frome-Westbury road.

Charlton N.E. of Malmesbury
680 de Cherletone 844 Cheltune, Choerletune 965–71 æt Ceorlatunæ 1086 Cerletone 1268 Cherleton

Places called Charlton usually grew up as outlying settlements dependent on a nearby town, in this case Malmesbury. OE *ceorla-tun* thus indicated an outlying farmstead inhabited by the lord's ceorls. A 'churl' was a man without rank or a free peasant.

Charlton (Charlton St Peter) S.W. of Pewsey
1198 Cherlinton 1225 Cherleton, Cherlentona 1368 Charleton by Uphaven

See CHARLTON, above. This village was dependent on Rushall. The church was dedicated to St Peter by 1308, though probably dates from the 12th century or earlier. The saintly suffix is now rarely used.

Charlton S. of Salisbury
1249 Cherleton 1311 Sherletone 1412 Charlton 1428 Charleton

See CHARLTON, above. Dependent on Downton.

Charlton E. of Shaftesbury
1216 in Cherleton

See CHARLTON, above. Dependent on Shaftesbury.

Chedglow N. of Malmesbury
956 Chegghemwllesbroke 1086 Chegeslaw, Chegeslei 1168 Cheggeslawa 1194 de Seggelawe 1203 Chichelewe 1257 Chigelawee 1300 Chaggely 1361 Chechelaw 1540 Chegislow 1587 Chedglo 1670 Chedslowe

The first element is most likely the personal name *Cecce*, as recorded in an Anglo-Saxon charter, the whole name meaning 'Cecce's funeral mound or barrow' (OE *hlaw*). The 956 version refers to a boundary stream.

Chelworth N.E. of Crudwell
c890 Cellanwurd 901 de Choellewrthe, Cellewird, Chellewrth 1065 Chellewrtha 1086 in Celeorde 1158 Cheleswurda 1281 Cheleworth juxta Magna Credewelle 1322 Chilworth 1773 Challoth

Evidently this OE *Ceolan-weorth*, 'Ceola's farmstead'. Earlier forms are hard to distinguish from CHELWORTH, below. *Magna Credewelle* is CRUDWELL.

Chelworth S.W. of Cricklade
c970 æt Ceolæswydae 1086 Celewrde 1130 Celesworda 1229 Chedeleswurthe 1272 Chellewrth 1334 Great Cheleworth 1347 Magna Scheleworth 1485 Chelleworth

See CHELWORTH, above. The remains of a moat south of Braydon Lane possibly indicate the original nucleus of the village.

Cherhill (cherul) E. of Calne
1155 Ciriel 1156 Cheriel 1158 Ceriel 1235 Cyriel 1275 Churiel 1294 Churhull 1316 de Chyrrele 1428 Chyryell 1637 Cherrell

Speculation surrounds the true meaning of this British name, for the forms listed are too late to allow positive identification. The present 'hill' element is obviously a corruption of some earlier word in view of the unusual pronounciation, possibly the same one that occurs in BRIXTON DEVERILL and FONTHILL (ie. diminutive ending *-ial* or British 'fertile upland'). The first element is possibly British *caer*, 'fort or camp', referring to nearby Oldbury Castle, or it may be a stream-name similar to the Welsh *ceri*.

Cheverell, Great and **Little** S. of Devizes
1086 Chevrell 1103 Capreoleum 1175 Chiverell 1179 Cheverel Magna 1198 Cheverelles 1242 Chiverel Parva, Magna 1274 Great Chyverel 1301 Little Cheveroill

Longstaff suggests the OE plant-name, *chervil*, from which he claims KEEVIL is also derived. There are certain similarities to CHERHILL and BRIXTON DEVERILL, ie. 'fertile or cultivated upland region' (the villages are high on the greensand ridge at the northern edge of Salisbury Plain). A connection has also been suggested with the Middle Welsh word *kyuar*, 'common-ploughed land'. The 1103 Latin version derives from a mis-translation based on the French word *chevreuil*, 'goat or roebuck'. The stream now called the Cheverell rises from the hillside to the south, and forms the boundary between the two parishes. Cheverell Magna and Parva are still used in a parochial context.

Chicklade N. of Hindon
c912 Cytlid 1199 de Chikelad 1211 Ciclet 1275 Chyclet 1297 de Chikelede 1300 Chitlad 1409 Chekelade 1491 in Chykelade

Probably from OE *Cices-lade*, 'Cice's road or trackway', although Ekwall suggests *cet-hlid*, 'gate into the wood', ie. the Great Ridge.

Chilhampton (chillington) N. of Wilton
1195 Childamptun' 1202 Chilhamton 1203 Childhampton 1500 Chellyngton

Cilda-ham-tun, 'the young man's homestead'. *Cilda* was probably a personal name given to a young man. See also DITCHAMPTON, NETHERHAMPTON and QUIDHAMPTON, which are also near Wilton.

Chilmark E. of Hindon
c930 æt Chieldmearc 984 cigel marc 1086 Chilmerc 1195 Childmerke 1289 Chelesmerke 1297 Chilemark 1302 Chylmerk 1306 Chilmark

The first element is either *Cilda*, as in CHILHAMPTON, or the WS word *cigel*, meaning 'peg or pole'. The ending is *mearc*, 'boundary or landmark'. Thus, 'boundary marked by poles' is the likeliest meaning.

Chilton Foliat N.W. of Hungerford
1086 Cilletone 1167 Cilton Roberti Foliot 1227 Chilton Foliot 1321 Chilton Tois 1332 Chilton Tieys 1336 Chilton Tyeis

The first word is probably OE *Cillan-tun*, 'Cilla's farmstead', although Longstaff puts forward OE *cyli*, 'well or spring', for the first element. The *Foliots* were a French family who also held the manor of DRAYCOT FOLIAT; their lineage had been replaced by that of the *Tyes* family by 1300.

NEW HALL AND CHEESE-MARKET, CHIPPENHAM.

Chippenham
878 Cippanhamme 880/5 Schyppenam 930 Cyppan hamm 940

Chippenham 1086 Chepeham 1155 Cheppeham 1200 Chipeham 1240 Sypeham 1250 Chuppeham 1319 Shippenham 1541 Chippyngham

OE *Cyppan-hamm*, descriptive of an enclosed water-meadow owned by *Cyppa*. The town grew up on a spur of land by the River Avon, enclosed by water on three sides. See also BREMILHAM. When the Danish forces captured Chippenham in 878, it was already established as a royal hunting lodge and an important residence of the Saxon kings.

Chirton (churton) S.E. of Devizes
1086 Cheritone 1196 Cherint' 1230 Chiriton 1279 Cheryton 1316 Churughton 1332 Churyggethon 1428 Shirghton 1481 Cherghton

Possibly OE *cirice-tun*, 'farmstead by the church'. The present church dates back at least to the 12th century. Or the first element may be similar to that in CHERHILL. Known locally as Cherrington until the 19th century.

Chisbury S.W. of Marlborough
1086 Cheseberie 1166 Chisseberia 1247 Chessebure 1270 Chysebiry 1279 Chessebury 1285 Chusseburia

Originally OE *Cissan-byrig*, 'Cissa's *burh* or fortified place'. Chisbury is a Saxon fortification, constructed during the reign of King Alfred after the establishment of Danelaw. Other *burhs* in Wiltshire which date from the same period are at CRICKLADE, MALMESBURY and WILTON. Cissa's name is also commemorated in Chichester (Hampshire), which he created capital of the South Saxon kingdom.

Chiseldon (Chisledon) S. of Swindon
c880 æt Cyseldene, at Kyseldene 891 Ciseldenu 901 Ceolseldene 1086 Chiseldene 1242 Cheselden 1281 Chuseldene 1353 Cheasledeane

Although the village lies on a prominent down, the name incorporates OE *denu*, 'valley', rather than *dun*, 'hill', preceded by WS *ceosel, cisil*, meaning 'gravel or shingle'. Hence, 'gravel valley', with reference to the steep coombe to the north-west of the church.

Chisenbury, West and **East** N. of Enford
1086 Chesigeberie 1202 Chesingbiria 1227 Chisiugebur 1275 Chesingbir' Prioris, Chesingbir' Foyle 1289 West, Estchesyngebur' Edw.I Chusyngbury 1493 Chesyngbury 1689 Chisonbury Dallyfolly

Either OE *Cissinga-byrig*, 'burh or fort of Cissa's people' (see CHISBURY), or OE *cisinga-byrig*, 'fort of the dwellers on the gravel' — the villages stand on the gravel terrace of the Salisbury Avon. East and West Chisenbury are on the east and west banks of the river respectively. Roger *de la Foyle* held the manor during the 13th century. The priory, which still stands at East Chisenbury, had connections with the priory at Ogbourne which was founded in the 12th century.

Chitterne E. of Heytesbury
1086 Chetre 1166 Cettra 1268 Chytterne 1289 Chuterne 1324 Chitterne Maiden 1428 in Chitterne, Cettre Beate Marie 1542 Chyttern

A difficult name to interpret, possibly meaning 'dwelling in or by the wood', from British *ceto* and OE *ærn*. Or the first element may be the same as in CHITTOE, the personal name *Cetta*. The western part of the village was formerly Chitterne St Mary, and the eastern part was Chitterne All Saints (also known as Upper Chitterne), after the two parish churches. However, only the chancel remains of St Mary's, and the parish names are rarely used today.

Chittoe (chitoo) S.W. of Calne
1167 de Chetewe 1226 Cheteweie 1263 Chutuwe 1330 Chitumersche 1375 Chuteweheye 1409 Chitue 1634 Chittoe

Possibly OE *Cettan-weg*, 'Cetta's way or track'. As the village lies within the bounds of the old Pewsham Forest, the first element may be the British word *ceto*, 'wood'. The marsh referred to in 1330 still lies to the north of the village.

Cholderton E. of Amesbury
1086 Celdrintone, Celdretone 1170 Childreton 1174 Cheldrintona 1270 Cheldrington 1316 Chaldrynton 1656 Choldrington

Ceolredinga-tun, 'the farmstead of Ceolred or Ceolric's people'.

Christian Malford N.E. of Chippenham
937 Cristemaleford 1086 Cristemeleforde 1166 Cristesmeleford 1316 Cristemalleford 1428 Crystmaelford

From OE *Cristes-mæl-ford*, which literally means 'the ford by Christ's mark' or 'ford by the cross'. Longstaff records that the steps and shaft of the old stone village cross once stood here.

Chute (shoot) N.E. of Ludgershall
1086 Cetum 1178 Ceit 1231 Chet 1235 Cett' 1289 Chuyt 1297 Cheote 1307 Chut

This is a Celtic name which probably derives from the word *ceto*, 'woodland': see PRESHUTE. Chute Forest was a continuation of SAVERNAKE Forest along the Wiltshire/Hampshire boundary. All the above forms, with the exception of 1235 and 1307, refer to the forest rather than the village of Chute. *Shoot* or *shute* is also a dialect word for a steep, narrow path or a precipitous descent, possibly descriptive of the lane leading towards Chute Causeway.

Clarendon E. of Salisbury
1072 Clarendun 1130 Clarendona 1279 at Claryndone 1315 Claryngdon

Probably *Claringa-dun*, 'hill of Clara's people', although Ekwall suggests OE *clæfren-dun*, 'clover-grown hill'. Clarendon Palace was built as a hunting-lodge for William the Conqueror in the days when the Royal Forest of Clarendon extended southwards to the boundary with Hampshire.

Clatford W. of Marlborough
1086 Clatford 1166 Clacford Monachorum 1622 Clatford Prioris

Clate was the OE word for goose-grass. Hence, 'ford where this plant grows'. There was a small priory here, a cell of the Abbey of St Victor en Caux in France. The stone-lined surface of the original ford can still be seen on the bed of the Kennet, immediately east of the bridge which now carries the lane from Clatford to the Bath road.

Clench S. of Marlborough
1289 Clenche 1330 Cleynche 1354 Clench

One possibility is that the name derives from an old word for the crowfoot plant, which grows here. Ekwall's theory is that *clench* is a dialect word for a lump or mass, referring to the prominent hill to the east of the village.

Clevancy N.E. of Calne
1086 Clive 1231 in Clive Wauncy 1316 de Clyve Wauncy 1428 Clyve Auncy 1580 Cleveansey

From OE *clif*, with reference to the steep escarpment here. See BUPTON and CLYFFE PYPARD. Robert *de Wauncy* held lands in the parish during the 13th century.

Clyffe Pypard S. of Wootton Bassett
983 æt Clife 1086 Clive 1230 in Clive Pipart 1242 Cliva Pipard 1282 Pippardesclyve 1284 Pypardesclive 1332 Clivepipard 1570 Cleve Pepper

See CLEVANCY, which is nearby. Richard *Pipart*, or Pipard, held the manor in 1231.

Coate E. of Devizes
1255 Cotes 1289 la Cote 1490 Cotes

From OE *cotan*, meaning simply 'group of cottages'.

Codford St Mary and **Codford St Peter** S.E. of Heytesbury
901 codan ford 1086 Coteford c1167 Cutiford 1282 Est Codeford 1310 Westcodeford 1428 Codeford Sancti Petri, Codeford Sancte Marie

From OE *Codan-ford*, 'Coda's or Codda's ford'. The ford over the Wylye is at Codford St Mary. Formerly called East and West Codford, St Mary and St Peter are the respective church dedications.

Colerne (culurn) W. of Corsham
1086 Colerne 1156 Culerna 1177 Culerne 1270 Cullerne 1330 de Colorne 1585 Collarne

Probably OE *Culan-ærn*, 'the household of Cula': see CHITTERNE, which has a similar second element. However, as Colerne stands on the hillside above the steep coombe formed by the By Brook, the first element may be derived from the Welsh word *col*, descriptive of a peak or summit.

Collingbourne Ducis and **Collingbourne Kingston** N. of Ludgershall
903 Colengaburnam 921 at Colingburne 1086 Colingeburne, Coleburna, Coleburne 1228 de Colyngneburna minori 1256 Colingburn' Comitis 1268 Colyngeborne Valence, Abbotes Colingburne 1289 Colyngeborn Abbatis 1306 Colingeburne Kingeston 1323 Colyngburn Valence 1507 Colyngbourne ducis 1509 Colyngborne strete

From *Colinga-burna*, 'stream of Colla or Cola's people' (see also CALCUTT), referring to the local stream now called the Bourne. The name of Collingbourne was perhaps originally applied to the whole of the upper Bourne valley (see WINTERBOURNE DAUNTSEY). Collingbourne Ducis, or Lower Collingbourne, was formerly a holding of the Earls of Leicester (hence the suffix *Comitis*) and was also held in the 13th century by the family of William *de Valence*, who also held SWINDON. *Strete* refers to the straggling nature of the village along the main thoroughfare. Collingbourne Kingston was once the property of the King and was named *Abbatis* because it was a holding of the Abbot of St Peter's, Winchester. The first DB entry refers to Ducis, the other two to Kingston.

Compton N.W. of Enford
c1080 of Cuntune 1086 Contone 1256 Cumpton 1329 Compton

OE *cumb-tun*, descriptive of the farmstead in a small valley.

Compton Bassett N.E. of Calne
1086 Contone 1182 Comtona 1228 Cumptone Basset

See COMPTON, above. Distinguished by the name of the medieval Lords of the Manor. Gilbert *Basset* was tenant here in 1233, Fulke *Basset* in 1242, both members of the same family that held WINTERBOURNE BASSETT and WOOTTON BASSETT.

Compton Chamberlayne W. of Wilton
1086 Contone 1208 Cumpton 1316 Compton Chamberleyne

See COMPTON, above. Robert *Camerarius* held the manor in 1208, and it passed to Geoffrey *le Chaumberleng* soon afterwards. *Camerarius* is a Latinised form of the surname.

Conock (cunnick) S.E. of Devizes
1211 Cunet 1242 Kunek 1316 de Coneke 1372 Connok

Probably derived from the Celtic word *cnoc*, also found in KNOOK, which means 'rounded hill or knoll'. The village stands on a very slight hill.

Coombe S. of Enford
1279 de Combe 1329 Coumbe

OE *cumb*, 'small valley'.

Coombe Bissett S.W. of Salisbury
1086 Cumbe, Come 1167 Cumba Maness' Biset 1288 Coumbe Byset super Ebelesburne 1385 Combebysset 1402 de Coumbe Byset 1639 Combissett

From OE *cumb*, 'small valley'. Tenant in 1167 was Manasser *Biset*, steward to Henry II. The 1288 form refers to the river Ebble rather than the village of Ebbesbourne, and can be interpreted as 'Coumbe-on-Ebelesburne'.

Corsham W. of Chippenham
1001 Coseham 1086 Cosseham 1160 Corsham 1185 Cosham 1196 Cossam 1201 Corsholm

Probably *Cosan-ham*, 'home of Cosa or Cusa', although Longstaff suggests that the first element may derive from the Cornish word *cos*, 'wood'. *Ham* is a special English word with the primary meaning of 'home', but can also be used to describe a dwelling-place, village or manor. Formerly called Corsham Regis as the King was chief tenant here at DB. The 'r' in the name is a later insertion due to local dialect.

Corsley W. of Warminster
1086 in Corselie 1166 Corselea 1190 Cosselega 1268 Corslee Magna 1369 Cossleye 1428 Parva Corslegh 1574 Estcorseley

Originally 'meadow by the marsh': *cors* is a Celtic word denoting reedy or boggy ground, in this case the land drained by the Rodden Brook. Little Corsley was also known as Corsley Kingston. The village lay within the Forest of Selwood until the Middle Ages.

Corston S. of Malmesbury
1065 Corstuna 1086 Corstone 1242 Coreston

'Farmstead in the marsh'. See CORSLEY, above. The marsh is drained by the Gauze Brook (Gauze is a corruption of *cors*).

Corton S. of Heytesbury
1086 Cortitone 1242 Cortone 1281 Westcortynton 1291 Cortyngton 1356 Estcorton

OE *Cortinga-tun*, 'the farmstead of Cort's people'. East Corton was the present Manor Farm, while West Corton describes West Farm and the present village. Known as Cortington until the last century.

Corton N.E. of Calne
1086 Crostone 1195 Corfton 1428 Corston

If the DB entry is accurate, this is probably OE *cros-tun*, 'farmstead by the gap', ie. in the chalk escarpment behind the manor.

Coulston, East and **West** S.W. of Devizes
1086 Covelestone, Cuuleston 1206 Coueleston 1484 Cowelston 1632 West Cowlston

Probably from the Saxon personal name, *Cufel* ('Cufel's farmstead').

Longstaff notes that the village was called *Coulestone Chaumberlayn* in 1316, after Simon and Nicholas Chamberlain, who owned lands here during the 14th century. See COMPTON CHAMBERLAYNE, also COWESFIELD. The two settlements of East and West Coulston now share the shortened name of Coulston.

Cowesfield S.E. of Salisbury
1086 Colesfelde, Cuulestone 1217 Cuvelesfeld 1272 Colneston Sturmy, Coleston Spileman, Coleston Loveraz 1319 Covelesfeld

From *Cufeles-feld*, 'Cufel's field or open space': see COULSTON. The family names refer to tenants of the estate during the Middle Ages.

Cricklade
904 ad Criccaladam c925 Crecca gelad c975 æt, into Cragelade 1086 de Crichelade 1196 Crekelade 1255 de Crikkelade 1311 Creyklade 1319 Kirikelade, Creeklade 1637 Cricklett

The variety of spellings for Cricklade in the Anglo-Saxon Chronicle (first three forms, above) indicate that the name is probably older than the Saxon language. Various other forms also occur on coins minted here during the later Saxon period. The second element is presumably OE *(ge)lad* or *lade*, 'passage or way', with reference to the crossing of the Thames and the Roman ford to the east of the town. Lechlade (Glos.) incorporates a similar ending. Possibilities for the first element include (a) OE *crecca*, 'creek', from Latin *crepido*, meaning 'a quay' or 'the walled edge of a river' — Cricklade was navigable from London until the late 18th century and was formerly used as an inland port for the Roman town of Cirencester; (b) Welsh *craig*, 'rock'; (c) Celtic *crich*, 'boundary'. In Saxon times the Thames marked the boundary between the kingdoms of Wessex and Mercia, so the Celtic element may refer to an earlier tribal boundary. After the introduction of Danelaw in the 9th century, a fortified *burh* was established at Cricklade by King Alfred as part of his defensive plans — other *burhs* in Wiltshire were at CHISBURY, MALMESBURY and WILTON.

Crockerton S. of Warminster
1249 Crokerton 1289 Crokeriston 1467 North Crokerton

From OE *croccera-tun*, 'potter's farmstead'. John *le Crocker* was resident here in 1268, Richard *le Poter* in 1252, both involved in the 13th century pottery industry which thrived in the village. Clay Hill and Potter's Hill are in the vicinity.

Crofton S.E. of Marlborough
1086 Crostone 1166 Croftun' 1194 in Corftoñ 1418 Crofton Brayboef 1428 Crofton

Assuming that the DB version is inaccurate, this is OE ***croft-tun***, 'farm with an enclosed croft'. William *Brayboef* held lands here in 1316.

Croucheston E. of Broad Chalke
1249 Crocheston 1289 Crukeston 1328 Crucheston 1374 Cryuchestone

The forms given are too late to say for sure what the first element means: it could be a personal name, or a corruption of either OE *cros*, 'cross', or Celtic *cruc*, 'hill or mound'. OE *tun*, 'farmstead', is the second element.

Crudwell N. of Malmesbury
854 at Croddewelle, at Criddanwylle 1065 Creddewilla 1086 Creduelle 1196 de Credewalle 1345 Estcruddewell 1353 Crodewelle 1428 Crudewell 1599 Curdwell

From a Celtic stream-name, rendered in OE as *Creodan-wielle*, 'Creoda's spring or stream'. Crudwell is situated at the head of Swill Brook, a tributary of the Thames. *Creoda*, the King of Mercia, was slain in the neighbourhood in 593. Longstaff records that there was formerly a well opposite the church called *Bery-well*. The present village was sometimes also known as East Crudwell to distinguish from the outlying manor of West Crudwell.

Cumberwell N. of Bradford
1086 Cumbrewelle 1232 Comerwell Hen.II. Cumberwella, Combreswell'

'Cumbra's well or spring' (OE *wielle*). *Cumbra* was probably the name of a Welshman.

Dauntsey S.E. of Malmesbury
850 Dometesig, Daunteseye, Damices eye 854 at Domeccesige 1086 Dantesie 1166 Danteseia 1257 Danteseye 1428 Dauntesey 1655 Dancy

Domices-ieg, 'Domice's marshy or well-watered land'. Dauntsey is on low land by the banks of the Avon. Ekwall suggests the personal name *Domgeat* for the first element.

Dean, West S.E. of Salisbury
c880 æt Deone 1086 Duene 1242 Dune 1270 Westdune 1275 Westden 1289 Doene 1310 Westdeene 1341 Deon 1345 Westdeone 1402 Deone

From OE *denu* or *dene*, 'valley'. Jones suggests origin from a Celtic word meaning 'sheltered or quiet spot'. The village is situated on an affluent of the Test, and is 'West' to differentiate from East Dean, which is in Hampshire. See also BRAYDON.

Deptford N.E. of Wylye
1086 Depeford 1242 Dupeford 1281 Duppeford 1341 Doepeford 1387 Deopeford 1428 Depeford 1630 Debtford

OE *deopa-ford*, 'the deep ford'. Deptford once stood on the northern bank of the Wylye, but today the river has swung southwards away from the village.

St. John's Church, Devizes

Devizes
1135–53 Divisas 1152 Divises 1227 Devizes 1330 Vises 1333 Dyvyses 1381 les Divyses 1462 Visez 1485 le Devisez

Devizes provides a good example of a medieval planned town. The castle at Devizes is first mentioned in 1106, although there are records of an earlier fortification on the site, which was destroyed by fire. The place-name is probably an English version of the old French word *devise*, 'boundary'. Devizes is thus 'at the boundaries', either between former Welsh territory and the lands of Wessex, or, more likely, between the manors of Potterne and Cannings, whose boundaries formerly passed through Devizes Castle. Medieval towns were traditionally sited at the boundaries of existing manors. To locals, the town is always 'Vize' or 'Vizes'.

Dilton Marsh S.W. of Westbury
1190 Dulinton 1221 in Dulton 1250 Dolton 1324 Dulton 1332 Mersshe 1535 Dylton 1638 Dilton le Marsh

Probably *Dyllan-tun*, 'Dylla's or Dulla's farmstead'. The original village of Dilton, with its ancient church and former mill on the River Biss, is now known as Old Dilton, having been eclipsed in size and importance by the 17th century settlement of Dilton Marsh to the north-west.

Dinton W. of Wilton
1086 Domnitone 1225 Dunyngton 1268 Donington 1305Donyngton 1505 Dynton

OE *Dunninga-tun*, 'farmstead of Dunna's people'. On the basis of the DB spelling, Longstaff favours a connection with Latin *dominus*, 'lord or master'.

Ditchampton (ditchington) N.W. of Wilton
1045 æt Dichæmatune 1086 Dechementon, in Dicehantone 1268 Dychehampton 1428 Dychampton

From OE *dic-hæme-tun*, 'farmstead of the dwellers by the ditch', referring to Grim's Ditch which runs north through Groveley Wood. See CHILHAMPTON.

Ditteridge (ditcheridge) W. of Corsham
1086 Digeric 1236 Dicherigga, Dicherug' 1283 Dychrugge 1376 Dykerigge 1428 in Dycherygge 1581 Dytchridge

'Dyke or ditch ridge' (from OE *dic-hyrcg*), which describes the spur of land overlooking the Bristol Avon, on which Ditchampton stands.

Donhead St Mary and **Donhead St Andrew** E. of Shaftesbury
871 Dunheued, Dunhefda 955 to Dun heafdan 956 Dunnynghefd 1086 Duneheve 1199 Dunneheued 1275 Dunhefde 1279 Donhaved c1290 Dunhef (de Sc̄e Marie) 1298 Donheved Sancte Marie 1302 Dounheved Sancti Andree 1345 Donehevede St.Andr' 1373 Donhed Andreu 1573 Over Donet, Nether Donet

Two distinct possibilities: either *dun-heafod*, 'head or top of the town'; or *don-heafod*, 'head of the Don', referring to a tributary of the Nadder which rises here. The 1573 versions refer to Donhead St Mary and Donhead St Andrew respectively.

Downton S. of Salisbury
672 Duntun 826 Dunton 948 in Duntune 1086 Duntone 1327 Dounton 1433 Estdounton

OE *dun-tun*, 'farm by the downland'.

Draycot Cerne N. of Chippenham
1086 Draicote, Dracote c1180 Draycotha 1228 Draycot 1345 Draicote Cerne 1394 Dreighcote Serne

Derived from OE *dræg*, indicative of a steep hill. The village lies to the west of a small hill. Hence, 'cottages by the hill or incline'. Henry *de Cerne*, Knight and Lord of *Draicot*, held the manor in 1225. His name indicates a connection either with Cerne in Dorset or the village of Cernay in eastern France.

Draycot Fitzpayne N.W. of Pewsey
1086 Draicote 1300 Draicot Rogeri Filii Pagani

See DRAYCOT CERNE. An old track leads northwards up the scarp slope to Draycot Hill. Roger *FitzPayne* held the manor in 1304. The 1300 form is a Latinised version of his name.

Draycot Foliat S. of Swindon
1086 Dracote 1197 Draicote 13th c. Dreicote Foliot 1308 Dreyckote Folyoht

See DRAYCOT CERNE. However, this hamlet stands on an open, treeless plateau away from any noticeable hill, so possibly the first element is OE *dreg, dryge*, 'dry'. Henry *Foliot* was tenant here in 1214. His family had been replaced by the Tyes by the end of the 13th century (see CHILTON FOLIAT). The sign at the farm spells the name as Draycott, without the suffix.

Dunkirk W. of Devizes

This name dates only from the 19th century, and was probably named by settlers from the Flemish port of Dunkerque. There are similarly-named places in Kent, Gloucestershire and Staffordshire.

Durley S.E. of Marlborough
1229 Durnley 1264 Durnelyghe 1278 Derley, Dirlay

OE *dierna-leah*, 'secret or hidden clearing', descriptive of its position in Savernake Forest. DURNFORD has a similar first element.

Durnford, Great and **Little** S. of Amesbury
1086 Diarneford, Darneford 1142 Derneford Sancti Andreæ 1158 Durneford c1220 Deorneford 1308 Great Durneford 1322 Durneford Parva 1412 Moche Durnford, Little Durnford 1540 Durnesford

From OE *dierna-ford*, 'the secret or hidden ford'. The ford was possibly by the orchard behind the church of St Andrew in Great Durnford, although there is no crossing of the Avon here now. Great Durnford was formerly Much Durnford (ME *moche*, 'great') also known as Hungerford Magna, after the family who once held it. John Evelyn wrote that Durnford was ". . . situate in a valley under ye plaine, most sweetly watered, abounding in trouts catched by speare in the night, when they come attracted by a light set in ye extreme of a boat".

Durrington N. of Amesbury
1086 Derintone 1178 Durenton 1215 in Durintone 1268 Hinedorintone 1270 Durentona, Hinedurintona 1286 Kingderinton, Hinderinton 1291 Duryngton 1389 Dyryngton

Originally *Dyringa-tun* or *Deoringa-tun*, 'the farmstead of the Dyrings or Deorings'. Durrington was made up of two old manors: *Kingderinton*, as the name suggests, was Crown property; *Hinderinton* was the land on the inside of the bend of the river Avon (ME *inne, hinne*, 'inside').

Eastcott S of Devizes
1167 Estcota 1349 Estcote 1500 in Estcote

OE *east-cot*, referring to this settlement of cottages to the east of LAVINGTON. The village is adjacent to EASTERTON.

Eastcourt N.E. of Malmesbury
901 de Escote 1065 Eastcotun 1222 de Estcote

See EASTCOTT, above. Lies due east of Crudwell. The suffix *-court* is a late substitution due to local dialect.

Easterton S. of Devizes
1412 Esterton Eliz.I Easterton Germons 1591 Easterton Garnham

This is a variant of EASTON, 'east farmstead', which taken at face value means 'more easterly farmstead'. The village lies east of LAVINGTON, towards EASTCOTT. Roger *Gernon* held the manor in 1242.

Easton E. of Shaftesbury
956 Estun 1249 in Eston

OE *east-tun*, 'east farmstead'.

Easton Grey W. of Malmesbury
1086 Estone 1268 Estuna 1289 Eston Grey 1311 Aston Gray 1316 de Estone Grey

See EASTON above. So-named possibly because it lies in the east of the parish of Sherston. John *de Grey* held the manor in 1243.

Easton Piercy N.W. of Chippenham
1086 Estone 1257 Eston 1304 Eston Peres 1559 Eston Peers al. Eston Pyers

See EASTON, above. The village is situated to the east of Yatton Keynell. The tenant in 1250 was Peter, or *Piers*, de Eston. Alternatively, the suffix may be taken from the name of a village called Percy near Caen in Normandy.

Easton Royal E. of Pewsey
1086 Estone 1232 Eston 1242 Aston 1268 Estone Prioris 1349 Easton

See EASTON, above. The village lies to the east of Milton Lilbourne. The King was chief tenant here at DB, and the eastern half of the parish included part of the royal estate of Savernake Forest. There was a small house of Austin Canons here in the 13th century.

Ebbesbourne Wake W. of Broad Chalke
672 on Ybbles burnan 826 Eblesburna 905 on Ebles burnan 1086 Eblesborne 1167 Ebleburn' Simonis Wach 1222 Ebeleborn 1271 Ebelesborne wak 1285 Ebelesburne Wake

The 672 reference to the local *burna*, or stream, includes the personal name *Ybbel* or *Ebbel*, ie. 'Ebbel's stream'. The river itself is now called the Ebble, and is thus a back-formation from the original Saxon personal name. Writing in the 16th century, Leland recorded the stream as *Chalkbourn*, probably because it flowed through BROAD CHALKE downstream from Ebbesbourne. Formerly a part of Cranborne Chase, Eblesbourne in medieval times would have described the whole upper part of the river. The manor was granted in 1205 to Galfridus, otherwise Jeffery, *de Wake*.

Edington E. of Westbury
878 to Ethandun 880/5 de Ethandune 968 Edyndon c1000 Ethandun 1086 in Edendone 1257 Edington 1428 Edyngton 1546 Eddington

Probably OE *Ethan-dun*, 'Etha's hill or down', although Ekwall puts forward *ethe-dun*, 'bare hill or down'. This was the site of King Alfred's decisive victory over Guthrum and the Danish forces in 878.

Elcombe S.W. of Swindon
1086 Elecombe 1168 Ellecumba 1179 Hellecumba 1250 Ellecumb

Probably OE *ellan-cumb*, 'elder-tree valley'. A headwater of the River Ray, called the Ely, rises in a deep coombe near Clouts Wood, so an alternative interpretation of the name could be *Ely-cumb*. Ely is a Celtic stream-name of unknown meaning, but with certain similarities to WYLYE. The name Elcombe is similar to *Ellandun*, the old name for the part of WROUGHTON where the parish church stands, overlooking Elcombe.

Elcot E. of Marlborough
1237 Elcot 1257 Ellecote 1402 in Elcote

Either *Ellan-cot*, 'Ella's cottages', or *ellan-cot*, 'cottage by the elder-tree'.

Elston N.W. of Amesbury
1086 Wintreburne 1168 Winterburn' Elye Giffard 1249 Elyston 1299 Wynterborne Eliston 1310 Eliston

One of several villages recorded as *Wintreburne* in DB: see BERWICK ST JAMES. The name was changed during the Middle Ages to avoid confusion, reaching its present form via the transitional *Wynterborne Eliston*. Elias *Giffard* held the manor in the 12th century, and the name is thus a post-Saxon *tun*-formation ('Elias's tun or farmstead'). See also BROUGHTON GIFFORD.

Enford N. of Amesbury
934 Enedford 1086 Enedforde 1200 Eneford 1540 Endeford

OE *ened-ford*, 'ford of the ducks', referring to a crossing-point of the Salisbury Avon.

Erlestoke S.W. of Devizes
c1200 Stokes 1227 Erlestok 1310 Littlestok 1325 Erlystok 1340 Eorlestoke 1517 Herrylstoke

OE *eorles-stoc*, 'the earl's stockaded place or settlement'. For a precise meaning of *stoc*, see BAVERSTOCK. Erlestoke once formed part of the parish of Melksham, which was held by Earl Harold at DB, hence the name. Earl Stoke was an alternative spelling prior to this century.

Etchilhampton (eshlington, ashelton) E. of Devizes
1086 Echesatingetone, Ecesatingetone 1196 Echehamt', de Ehelhamton' 1206 Hechesetingeton 1228 Hechelhamt' 1349 Ethelhampton 1622 Ashlington

Judging by the wide variety of forms, this is a name which has caused a few problems to scribes over the years. Etchilhampton possibly comes from *Eccelinga-tun*, 'the farmstead of Ecca's people'. Or the name may incorporate OE *ecels*, 'addition', denoting the additional land taken into cultivation when the village was developed, or the addition of Etchilhampton to the larger parish of ALL CANNINGS. Locally the village name is abbreviated to 'Etchel'.

Everleigh N.W. of Ludgershall
704 Eburleagh, Eburleah 1172 Everlai, Everlay 1265 Everle 1281 Everlegh 1296 Everley 1306 Est Everlee 1347 West Everlee 1563 Myddell Everley

From *Eoforan-leah*, 'clearing or meadow frequented by wild boar'. The village was within the old Forest of Chute, which explains the presence of boar. Lower Everleigh was formerly known as West Everleigh, while the area around the church was Middle Everleigh. The 704 references are taken from a charter of King Ine of Wessex.

Eysey (ayzi) N.E. of Cricklade
775/8 æt Eseg, Esig 855 æt Esege 1086 Aisi 1259 Esy 1428 Eysy

The first element is probably connected with the Roman name for the upper Thames, *Isis*. The second element is OE *ieg*, 'marshy land or islet', which well describes Eysey's low-lying position near the river.

Farleigh Wick N.W. of Bradford
1257 Farlegh Wyke 1393 Farleghwyke 1396 Farlewyk 1485 la Wyke

This was originally simply Wick, from OE *wic*, 'outlying dairy-farm'. The prefix was added to distinguish the village from other similarly-named places, and refers to nearby monkton farleigh.

Farley E. of Salisbury
1086 Farlege 1109/20 Fernelega 1198 Ferleg' 1227 de Farleye 1285 Farlegh 1287 Farnle

OE *fearn-leah*, 'fern or bracken clearing'. Formerly within the bounds of Buckholt Forest.

Faulston S.W. of Salisbury
1275 in Fallerstone 1305 Fallerdeston

This name seems to be a post-Saxon *tun*-formation, and indicates a settlement founded by a Frenchman named *Fallard*, who was a follower of the Conqueror.

Fifield S. of Enford
1086 Fifhide 1230 Fifide 1275 Fihide Episcopi 1297 Est Fifhide 1310 Parva Fifhide 1362 Langefifide 1494 Fyffhyde

A hide (OE *hid*) was a measure of land calculated to be large enough to support one family and their dependants, or as much land as could be tilled with one plough in a year — Fifield was thus composed of five hides. East Fifield was possibly an alternative name for the hamlet of COOMBE, which lies opposite Fifield on the eastern bank of the Avon. *Langefifide* was the old name for Longstreet, which lies towards Enford. 'Parva' is probably to distinguish the village from FYFIELD. Formerly a holding of the Bishop of Winchester.

Fifield Bavant W. of Broad Chalke
1086 Fifhide 1267 Fiffide Escudemor 1428 Fiffyde 1436 Fiffehyde Beaufaunt 1510 Fyfhed Bavent

See FIFIELD, above. According to DB, *it gelded for five hydes* at the time of Edward the Confessor. *Escudemor* is the Norman rendering of the family name Scudamore (see UPTON SCUDAMORE). Alesia *de Bavent* held the manor in 1301, taking her name from the French village of Bavent, near Caen. Other Wiltshire villages named after French places include ASHTON GIFFORD, EASTON PIERCY, LYDIARD TREGOZE, MILTON LILBOURNE, NEWTON TONY, STANTON ST QUINTIN and STOKE FARTHING. Today, Fifield is a delightful unsignposted hamlet on the banks of the infant river Ebble.

Figheldean N. of Amesbury
1086 Fisgledene 1115 Ficheldene 1157 Fykeldene 1285 Fyhelden 1320 Fygheldene 1324 Fyzelden 1572 Fyeldean 1640 Feildeane

From OE *Fygelan-denu*, 'Fygla's valley'.

Fisherton Anger near Salisbury
1086 Fiscartone 1242 de Fisserton 1279 Fisshelton 1324 Fissherton Aucher 1432 Fyssherton Aunger

From OE *fiscera-tun*, 'farmstead of the fisher-folk'. Fishing was the primary occupation of the villagers at the time of DB, and two professional fishermen are recorded as residents in the late 13th century. Richard *filius Aucheri*, 'son of Aucher', held the manor in 1242, his name subsequently being mis-spelt *Ancher* or *Anger*.

Fisherton de la Mere N.W. of Wylye
1086 Fisertone 1173 Fisserton 1275 Fiskerton 1318 Fissherton 1412 Fyssherton Dalamare

See FISHERTON ANGER, above. John *de la Mere* was tenant at this estate on the Wylye in 1375.

Fittleton S. of Enford
1086 Viteltone 1211 Fitletone 1220 Fetelton 1235 Fitelton 1275 Futelton 1303 Fitilton 1354 Fydelton

OE *Fitelan-tun*, 'Fitel's farmstead'. A Saxon thegn called *Vitel* is recorded as tenant here in 1066.

Fonthill Bishop and **Fonthill Gifford** (funtle) E. and S.E. of Hindon
901 Funtial, Funtgeall 977 Funteal 1086 Fontel 1166 Funtel' 1284 Funtele 1291 Fontel Giffard, Fontel Epi 1345 Fontelgyffard 1367 Fontel Episcopi Eliz.I Overfonthill

As can be seen from the earlier forms, this is not the *-hill* formation it appears to be on first sight. The second element is possibly the diminutive ending *-ial*, 'little', or a word meaning 'fertile upland': see CHERHILL and BRIXTON DEVERILL. OE *funt* describes a fountain or well, probably a nearby source of a short tributary of the Nadder. For *funt*, see also FOVANT and TEFFONT, which are also on tributaries of the Nadder. Denewulf, the Bishop of Winchester, obtained lands here in the 10th century, while the chief tenant in 1086 was Berenger *Gifard*. Fonthill Gifford was formerly known as Over or Upper Fonthill. Fonthill Bishop is also known locally as Bishop's Fonthill. The modern pronounciation of Fonthill is probably identical to the original Saxon pronounciation.

Ford N.E. of Salisbury
1086 Wintreburne 1189 Winterburneford 1320 Winterbourneford 1605 Ford

The Roman road from Old Sarum to Winchester formerly crossed the River Bourne here by means of a ford. See WINTERBOURNE BASSETT.

Fosbury S. of Hungerford
1086 Fosteberge, Fistesberie 1229 Upforstebury 1268 Forstebyri 1270 Forstebery 1290 Forestebur' 1368 Westeforstebury

OE *Forstan-byrig*, 'Forsta's *burh* or hillfort', referring to the large Iron Age hillfort called Fosbury Camp, which dates from about 150 BC.

Fovant (fuvant) E. of Tisbury
901 Fobbanfuntan, Fobbefunte 1086 Febefonte c1230 Fobhunte 1242 Fofunte 1302 Upfovent 1306 Ovre Foſhunte, Netherefoſhunte 1329 Foffonte 1428 Fovent

From an original OE *Fobban-funta*, 'Fobba's fountain, well or spring'. A tributary of the Nadder rises here, as at FONTHILL and TEFFONT. Longstaff suggests the first element may be OE *fob*, 'foam or froth'. Hence: 'foamy fountain'.

Foxham N.E. of Chippenham
1065 Foxham 1553 Voxham

OE *fox-ham*, indicating a settlement where foxes were common, or whose owner trapped foxes.

Foxley S.W. of Malmesbury
1086 Foxelege 1227 Foxlegh c1290 Foxle 1428 Foxele

'Lea or meadow frequented by foxes' (OE *fox-leah*). Alternatively, the first element may be a corruption of Fosse, after the Roman Fosse Way which runs to the west of the village.

Fresdon (Fresden) E. of Highworth
1263 Fersedon 1267 Fressindon 1307 Ferlslesdon 1365 Versshedon 1392 Frissheton

The second element is OE *dun*, 'hill'. The first element is either OE *fyrs* or *fersc*. Hence: 'furze-hill' or 'fresh-hill'.

Froxfield W. of Hungerford
804 Forscanfeld 1166 Frossefeld 1242 Froxfeld 1297 Vroxfeld c1300 in Frockesfeld 1377 Throxfeld

OE *forsca-feld*, 'field of frogs'. The stream here was recorded as *forsca burna* in a charter dated 778. The stream-name was subsequently applied to a field here, and eventually to the village.

Fugglestone St Peter E. of Wilton
1208 de Fuglestoñ 1236 Fughelistone 1256 Fuelestone 1280 Foleston 1346 Fougheleston 1540 Fouleston

OE *Fugules-tun*, 'Fugul's farmstead'. The personal name comes from the OE word *fugol*, meaning 'bird or fowl'. The 13th century church is dedicated to St Peter.

Fyfield W. of Marlborough
1086 Fifhide 1257 Fifhude c1290 Fifhide 1505 Fyfilde 1553 Phiphild 1558 Fyfelde

See FIFIELD. The village consisted of five hides at the time of the Domesday Survey.

Garsdon E. of Malmesbury
701 Gersdune 1066 Garsduna 1086 Gardone 1281 Gevesdon c1290 Gevesindon 1428 Garesden 1512 Garrysdon 1675 Geersden

OE *gærs-dun*, 'grassy hill'.

Gastard S.W. of Chippenham.
1154 Gatesterta 1167 Getestert 1177 Gateherst 1428 Gastard 1601 Gadsteed

Possibly from a combination of OE *gat*, 'she-goat', and *steort*, 'tail of land'. The second element also occurs in STERT.

Goatacre S.W. of Wootton Bassett
1242 Godacre 1348 Gatacre 1408 Gotagre

OE *gat-æcre*. Literally 'goat-acre'.

Gomeldon (gumeldun) N.E. of Salisbury
1189 Gomeledona 1279 Gomeldon, Gumeldon Edw.I in Gomeledon' 1289 Gomelesdon

OE *Gumelan-dun*, 'Gumela's hill'. There is a small but prominent hill to the east of the river Bourne.

Grafton, East and **West** S.E. of Marlborough
1086 Graftone, Grastone 1130 Graftona 1198 Est Graftone, West Graftone 1211 Greftone 1308 Westgraftone 1324 Graffton

Probably derived from OE *graf-tun*, 'farm by the grove'. An alternative meaning may be *groef-tun*, 'farm by the grave or trench'. The old local pronounciation was 'Gratton'.

Grimstead, East and **West** S.E. of Salisbury
1086 Gremestede, Gramestede 1160 Grenesteda 1186 Grimesteda 1245 de Grymstede 1249 Westgrimstede 1263 Gremsted 1269 Estgremsted 1287 Westgrmsteden, Estgrymstede

It has been suggested that Grimstead is so-called because of its proximity to Grim's Ditch (*956 grimes dic; 1352 Grymmesdich*), which ran northwards towards the Iron Age hillfort at Figsbury Ring. The name is thus OE *Grimes-stede*, 'Grim's place or settlement'. However, Ekwall's interpretation of the name as OE *grene-ham-stede*, 'green homestead', should not be ruled out.

Grittenham W. of Wootton Bassett
850 ad Gruteham 1065 Grutenham 1268 Gryteham c1290 Gruteham, Grucenham 1595 Gritnam 1602 Grittingham

The first element is either a personal name, *Grutel* or *Grytel*, or from OE *greot*, 'gravel'. Hence: 'Grutel's homestead' or 'gravelly homestead'. The village lies on an outcrop of Great Oolite. See also GRITTLETON.

Grittleton N.W. of Chippenham
940 at Grutelingtone 1086 Gretelintone 1241 Gridelington 1316 Gratelington 1330 Gritelyngton 1428 Gretelyngton, Grythyngton

Probably *Grytelinga-tun*, 'farmstead of Grytel's people'. Ekwall puts forward *greot-hlinc-tun*, meaning 'gravel-hill farmstead'. See also GRITTENHAM.

Grittleton: Old Manor House

Grovely and **Grovely Wood** (Groveley) N.W. of Wilton
940 grafan lea 1086 foresta de Gravelinges 1155 Graveninge 1167 Grauelea 1255 Gravelinch 1320 Graveley 1402 Grovelegh

Either *groefan-leah*, 'brushwood clearing', or *graf-leah*, 'clearing by the grove'. The name was probably applied first to a clearing in the wood and later to the wood itself. Grovely Wood is today much the same size as it was in medieval times.

Ham S. of Hungerford
931 æt Hamme, of Hame 1086 Hame 1166 Hama

The normal interpretation of this name would be OE *ham*, 'hamlet or home'. However, another possibility is OE *hamm*, which describes a piece of land in the bend of a river, in this case a small tributary of the Kennet.

Hampton S.W. of Highworth
1086 Hantone 1227 Hamton 1402 Hampton Turvyle

This name is probably OE *ham-tun*, 'homestead', although the DB spelling suggests *hean-tun*, 'high farmstead'. Robert *de Turneville* held the manor in 1279. See also SEVENHAMPTON.

Hanging Langford N.W. of Wilton
1242 Hangindelangeford 1257 Hanginge 1337 Honyngelangeford 1428 Hangyng Langeford

OE *langan-ford*, 'long or wide ford'. See STEEPLE LANGFORD. *Hanging* is a ME word which describes the steep valley slope overlooking the river Wylye where the village stands.

Hankerton N.E. of Malmesbury
680 de Hanekyntone 1065 Honekynton 1249 Haneketon 1399 Hankyngton 1428 Hanketon 1491 Hankerton

Hanecan-tun, 'Haneca's farmstead'. A Saxon charter refers to *hanan welle*, probably on a headwater of Swill Brook which marks the parish boundary.

Hannington W. of Highworth
1086 Hanindone 1211 Hanedon 1300 Hanyngdone 1324 Hanyndon 1428 Est Hanynton

Haninga-dun, 'hill or down of Hana's people'.

Hardenhuish (harnish) N.W. of Chippenham
854 Heregeardingc hiwisce 1086 Hardenhus 1177 Hardehiwis 1242 Herdenewiz 1291 of Hardene Hywich 1310 Hardenhiwisch 1410 Hardynghuwyssh 1568 Harden Hewysh al. Harnysh

Heregeardan-hiwisc, 'the hide or family holding of Heregeard'.

Harnham, East and **West** S. of Salisbury
c1115 Harnham 1130 Hareham 1206 Harinham Hen.III Estharnham

1230 Harham 1233 Harram 1275 Westharnam

OE *Haran-ham*, 'Hara's homestead'. The personal name derives from the OE word for a hare.

Hartham N.W. of Chippenham
1086 Heortham, Hertham 1196 Hortham 1202 Hertham

Heort-ham, 'home or enclosure of the hart, stag or deer'. A hart is a male red deer in its sixth year. The second element may however be OE *hamm*: see HAM.

Hatch, East and **West** S. of Hindon
Hen.I Hascia 1199 de Hache 1201 Heche 1225 Westhacha 1242 Esthache 1325 Weshacch c1380 East Hatch

Hatch lies in the thickly-wooded area to the west of Tisbury, the name deriving from OE *hæcc*, the word for an opening into a forest usually guarded by a gate or wicket.

Haxton N. of Amesbury
1172 Hakenestan 1212 Hakenestone 1268 Hakeleston 1286 Acleston 1454 Hakyston

The first element is probably the Scandinavian personal name *Hacun*, combined with either *tun* or *stan*. Hence: 'Hacun's farmstead or stone'. Known also as Hacklestone until the later 19th century.

Haydon and **Haydon Wick** N.W. of Swindon
1242 Haydon 1249 Haydonwyk 1268 Wykeheydon c1290 de Heydone 1379 Haidon 1428 in Haydoneswyke

Haydon is *heana-dun*, 'high down', or *heg-dun*, 'hay-down'. Wick denotes the outlying farm attached to the estate of Haydon. Haydon Wick, as a suburb of Swindon, has since eclipsed the original settlement of Haydon in size and importance.

Hazelbury N. of Bradford
1001 at Heselberi 1086 de Haseberie 1189 Haselberga 1300 Haselberwe 1324 Hasselbury

Hæsel-berie, 'open field where the hazel-trees grow'. Hazels often grew as forest undergrowth and had many uses: hazel-rods were used to make hurdles, while Cobbett in 1826 recorded the harvest of hazelnuts in Wiltshire.

Hazeldon S.W. of Tisbury
1199 Haselden Edw.I in Haselden' 1378/84 Hazeldon 1382 Haseldenefeld 1493 Hasilden

Despite the present spelling, the second element is in fact OE *denu*, 'valley', judging by the earlier forms. The name is thus OE *hæsel-denu*, 'hazel-valley', descriptive of this hamlet's position on the valley slope beside the river Sem. Hazeldon stands on the northern edge of Cranborne Chase in an area which is thick with hazel-woods.

Heddington N. of Devizes
1086 Edintone 1203 Hedinton 1212 Heddenton 1237 Hedlintun 1307 Hedynton 1403 Hedyngton Cantelo

Hedinga-tun, 'farmstead of Hedde's or Hodda's people'. Longstaff notes that *Hedda* was Bishop of Wessex in 676. See also HODSON. Robert *de Cantilupp* held the manor in 1316.

Heytesbury
1086 Hestrebe c1115 Hegtredebiri 1183 Heichtredeberi 1194 Hichtresdesberia c1290 Heghtredebury 1328 Westheghtredebury, Istheghtredbury 1445 Haitesbury 1533 Heytysbury

The personal name which makes up the first part of Heytesbury is obscure, and may be either *Hegtred*, the Scandinavian *Estred* or a woman's name, *Heahthryth*. The second element is OE *byrig*, denoting the *burh* or fortified place of this person. Longstaff interprets the name as 'high-tree-down'. Also spelt Haytesbury until recent years.

Heywood N. of Westbury
1225 Heiwode 1241 Heywud 1268 Hewode

Heaga-wudu, 'hedged or fenced woodland'. Clanger and Picket Woods are the remnants of the old Forest of SELWOOD. See also HAYDON WICK for an alternative first element.

Highway N.E. of Calne
1086 Hiwi, Hiwei 1153 Heiewei 1219 Hywey, de Yweye 1232 Hyweie 1289 Hegheweye

At first sight this seems to be OE *heah-weg*, 'highway', but this is unlikely as the village lies far from any major roads. Nor does 'high' refer to Highway's altitude, as it lies directly at the foot of the Lower Chalk escarpment. Another possibility is OE *heg-weg*, 'hay-way'.

Highworth
1086 de Wrde 1094 Wortha 1158 Wrdha 1232 Hegworth 1234 Hauteworth 1257 Alta Whorth 1281 Heyghewrthe 1388 Hieworth 1428 Hyworth

Originally known simply as Worth, from OE *weorth*, 'farmstead'. The prefix *High-* seems to have been added during the 13th century to describe the town's position on the prominent Corallian ridge overlooking the upper Thames valley. The 1234 form shows Norman influence, while the 1257 is partly Latinised.

Hilcott (illkit) W. of Pewsey
1196 in Hulcote 1236 de Hulcote 1242 Hulkot' 1249 Hullecote

OE *hyll-cote*, 'cottages on the hill'. Or possibly the first element is *hulu*, meaning 'shed or hovel'.

Hill Deverill S. of Warminster
1086 Devrel 1130/5 Hull 1202 Hulla 1227 Hulle Deverel 1324 Hulledeverel

From *hyll*, the OE word for a hill. Hill Deverill lies downstream from BRIXTON DEVERILL.

Hilmarton N. of Calne
962 Helmerdingtun 1086 Adhelmertone, Helmerintone, Helmertune 1198 Helmerton 1349 Hilmerton

Helmheardinga-tun, 'the farmstead of Helmheard's followers'. The first DB entry incorporates the Latin prefix *ad*, 'to, towards'.

Hilperton N.E. of Trowbridge
1086 Helprinton, Helperitune 1232 Hulprinctona 1268 Hylperton 1279 Hulpringtun 1415 Hylprington 1428 Hulpurton, Hulprynggton

OE *Helpricinga-tun*, 'the farmstead of Helpric's people'.

Hindon E. of Shaftesbury
1249 Hendon 1268 Hynedone 1281 Hyndon 1411 Esthindon, Hyndown

Possibly *heana-dun*, 'high down', but more likely *higna-dun*, 'down or hill belonging to a religious or secular household'. Hindon is a planned settlement, laid out by the Bishop of Winchester in the 13th century at the meeting-place of several ancient routes. See also HINTON PARVA.

Hinton, Great (henton) E. of Trowbridge
1216 Henton' 1316 Henton 1547 Great Henton

High farm. See BROAD HINTON. The village lies on the edge of the Corallian ridge, and is 'Great' to distinguish from HINTON PARVA.

Hinton Parva or **Little Hinton** E. of Swindon
854 Hynyton 12th c. Hynyton 1242 Hineton 1244 Hyniton 1300 Hyneton 1311 Little Hynyngton

Of similar derivation to HINDON. The manor formerly belonged to the monks of Winchester. The Latinised name of Hinton Parva dates from the 17th century, and distinguishes the village from either HINTON, GREAT or BROAD HINTON. The village signs give both forms of the name, although Little Hinton is locally less common.

Hippenscombe N.E. of Ludgershall
1231 Heppingcumb 1257 Huppanghescumb 1292 Hippingescumbe 1371 Ippingescombe

Hippinges-cumb, 'Hyppa's coombe or small valley'. *Heppo* is a recorded personal name in DB.

Hodson S. of Swindon
901 Hordestan, Horeston *1222 Hodeston* *1249 Hoddeston*

The 901 forms indicate that this is OE *horde-stan*, 'stone where a hoard or treasure is hidden'. Aubrey records that the village name was 'formerly spelled *Horderes-tun* or *Hoddeston'*. Alternatively, this is *Hodes-tun*, 'Hodd's farm'.

Holt N. of Trowbridge
1242 Holt, Holte *1257 la Holte* *1316 de Holte*

Holt was the OE word for a wood or copse. In 1252 Robert *de Holt* was granted free warren in the demesne lands of his manor of Holt.

Homington S.W. of Salisbury
956 humming tun *1086 Humitone* *1130 Humintona* *1244 Hommynton*

Huminga-tun, 'Humma's farmstead'. Humma derives from the OE personal name *Hunbeald*.

Hook N. of Wootton Bassett
1238 la Hok, la Hoke *1310 le Hoke* *1327 le Houk, Houke*

From OE *hoc*, denoting a corner or nook. The village is situated on a well-marked spur of land, or perhaps the name refers to a spur of Bradon Forest. *Hook* is also a Wiltshire dialect word for 'a corner of land taken into cultivation'.

Horningsham S.W. of Warminster
1086 Horningesham, Horningham *1115 Hornigesham* *1242 Ornigesham* *1289 Magna Hornynggesham* *1390 Little Hornyngesham* *1405 Hornesham*

Horninges-ham, 'Horning's homestead'. The personal name probably comes from the uncomplimentary OE noun *hornung*, meaning 'bastard'. Little Horningsham lay to the south of the present village.

Horton N.E. of Devizes
1158 Hortona *1203 Horton* *1220 Hortone*

OE *horh-tun*, 'dirty farmstead', from OE *horu*, meaning 'dirt or mud'. The village is on the low-lying Greensand of the Pewsey Vale, near a headwater of the Salisbury Avon.

Huish (yewish) S.W. of Marlborough
1086 Iwis *1162 Hiwis* *Hen.III Iwys* *1291 Huwes* *1331 Hywysshe* *1494 Hwys*

From OE *hiwisc*, 'a holding of land on which a household is settled'. See HARDENHUISH. The village grew up in an early clearing of Savernake Forest. More commonly spelled Hewish during the last century.

Hullavington (hullington) S.W. of Malmesbury
1086 Hunlavintone 1203 Hundlavington 1330/5 Hullavington 1422 Hundlaunton 1645 Hull Lavington

Hunlafinga-tun, 'farmstead of Hunlaf's people'. *Hunlaf* was a common OE personal name.

Hurdcott W. of Wilton
1086 Hardicote 1242 Hurdecote 1249 Herdecote 1659 Hurcott

Either OE *heord-cote*, which taken literally means 'flock-cottage, or more likely *heorda-cote*, 'herdsman's cottage'.

Hurdcott N.E. of Salisbury
1086 in Herdicote 1332 Hurdecote

See HURDCOTT, above.

Idmiston S.E. of Amesbury
947 ắt Idemestone 1189 Idemestona 1268 Ydomeston, Idemereston c1280 Ydemiston 1305 Edemeston 1316 de Idemistone

'Idhelm's or Idmær's farmstead'.

Imber N.E. of Heytesbury
1086 Imemerie 1146 Immemera 1200 Himmemere 1242 Ymmemere 1290 Imere 1324 Ynmere 1428 Inmere 1435 Immer al. Hymbemer

Probably OE *Imman-mære*, 'Imma's boundary or landmark', possibly referring to a boundary between two local hundreds. Alternatively, the second element may refer to a local pool.

Inglesham N. of Highworth
c950 æt Inggeneshamme c970 Incgenaesham 1160 Inglesham 1190 Englesham 1198 Ynglesham 1279 Overenglesham 1291 Inglesham

OE *Ingeldes-hamm*, 'Ingeld's or Inga's hamm or enclosed meadow', in this case the land on the inner bend of the river Thames, which forms the parish and county boundaries. Upper Inglesham was formerly known as Over Inglesham.

Ivy Church S.E. of Salisbury
1109/20 Monasterium Hederosum 1155 Capella Ederosa 1242 Ivichurch, Ivechirch 1246 Ivychurch 1461 Yvechurche

Ivy Church was a former Augustinian priory. The present name seems to derive from a mis-translation of the Latin *Monasterium Hederosum*, which literally means 'monastery covered with ivy'. The absence of earlier forms does not allow us to discover any Saxon nomenclature which may have been in use prior to the 12th century.

Keevil E. of Trowbridge
964 on Kefle wirtrim 1130 Chivelai 1205 Kivelia 1240 Kyvelegh 1316 de Kyvele 1318 Keyvele 1362 Keivele 1546 Kevell

There are two main possibilities for the first element: either the OE personal name, *Cyfa*, or OE *cyfel* (from *cyf*, 'tub or vessel'), descriptive of the depression in which Keevil lies. The second element is obscure, although the forms prior to the 14th century suggest OE *leah*, 'clearing or meadow'. Longstaff puts forward the plant-name, chervil or cerfille, which is apparently common in the locality. The 964 form includes the OE word *wyrtruma*, 'boundary'. See also CHEVERELL.

Kellaways N.E. of Chippenham
1226 Cailleway 1304 Caillewey 1585 Keylewayes

Probably derived from the French family name. Held by William *de Caillewey*, and by Elias *de Kaillewey* in 1227. Originally part of the manor of TYTHERTON.

Kennett, East and **West** W. of Marlborough
939 on Cynetan 1086 in Chenete 1220 Kenete 1267 Eskenette 1288 Westkenete 1332 Estkynet

Kennett is derived from a Celtic river-name equivalent to *Cunetio* or *Cunetione*, the old Roman name for MILDENHALL, and is also found in Kintbury (Berkshire). The precise meaning is obscure, although Ekwall interprets it as 'exalted or holy river', with reference to a pre-Christian river deity. The 939 version refers to the river Kennet, while the others all refer to the parish. *Chenete* is recorded three times in DB. Note the modern spelling of Kennet for the river and Kennett for the villages.

Kilmington N.E. of Mere
1086 Chelmetone, Cilemetone 1251 Culminton Hen.III Kulmeton 1403 Kylmyngton

Probably OE *Cynehelma-tun*, 'Cynehelm's farmstead'.

Kingston Deverill N.E. of Mere
1086 Devrel 1206 in Kingesdeverell 1236 Dewrelquinston 1282 Kyngeston Deverel

See BRIXTON DEVERILL, which lies downstream of this village. The 13th century versions denote that this was Crown property after the Norman Conquest. Kingston appears to be a post-Saxon *tun*-formation, and is not derived from an original OE *cyninges-tun*.

Kington Langley N. of Chippenham
1086 Langhelei 1189 Langela 1289 Northlangele 1636 Langley Kington

Langan-leah, 'long clearing or meadow'. Kington Langley was formerly Crown property, also known as North Langley to distinguish from LANGLEY BURRELL. The part of the manor now known as Fitzurse Farm was originally called Langley Fitzurse, and was held at the Conquest by *Urso*.

Kington St Michael N. of Chippenham
934 Kingtone 1086 Chintone 1174/91 Chinctuna 1189 Kinctona 1244

Kingtun 1279 Kyngton Michel 1281 Kynton Mich'is 1321 Munchenekyngton 1327 Estkington 1428 Kyngton Michaelis 1503 Michells Kynton

OE *cyne-tun*, 'royal farmstead'. Like KINGTON LANGLEY, this was Crown property before the Norman Conquest. St Michael is the dedication of the parish church. *Munchene* (from OE *mynecunu*, 'nun') would be translated today as 'Monkton' and refers to St Mary's Priory, an ancient Benedictine nunnery which was founded here in the 12th century. From its connections with Glastonbury Abbey, the village was sometimes known as Kington Monachorum, or *Moyne*. 'East' in relation to KINGTON, WEST.

Kington, West N.W. of Corsham
1086 Chintone 1195 Westkinton 1211 Westkingtoñ 1322 West Cyngton 1468 Westkynington 1607 West Keynton

This village is 'West' to distinguish from KINGTON ST MICHAEL, formerly East Kington.

Knighton E. of Broad Chalke
955 cnihta ford, cnita land 1200 Knichteton, Cnicteton 1322 Knyghteton

OE *cneohta-tun*, 'farmstead of the household servants or knights',. A half-knight's fee was held here by Joan de Nevill. *cnihta ford* refers to a crossing of the river Ebble.

Knook (nuk) S.E. of Heytesbury
1086 Cunuche 1107 Cnuca 1220 Cnuk 1249 Knuch 1314 Cnouk 1332 Knouke 1496 Chenuka

Knook comes from the Celtic *cnoc*, equivalent to the modern Welsh *cnwc*, meaning 'lump or hillock'. There is a tumulus south of the river towards Corton, or the name may describe the prominent Knook Horse Hill. See CONOCK, which is of similar derivation.

Knoyle, East and **West** W. of Hindon
948 æt Cnugel 984 Cnugellege 1086 Chenvel 1228 Stepelknoel' 1275 Knowel c1290 Cnoel Magna, Cnoel hodierne 1346 Knowell Episcopi 1408 Little Knoyell 1428 Knoel Parva 1467 Esteknoyle, Westeknoyle

Knoyle is probably derived from a Celtic word similar to that which gave its name to KNOOK, equivalent to the Welsh *cnol* and OE *cnugel*, meaning 'knuckle, knoll or rounded hill'. East Knoyle was formerly *Stepelknoel*, a reference either to its church or to the market (OE *stapul*). It was also known as Knoyle Magna as it is the larger of the two villages, and *Knowell Episcopi* as it was a holding of the Bishop of Winchester. In more recent years, the latter name was rendered as Bishop's Knoyle. Longstaff also records Knoyle Regis as a former name for East Knoyle, which was held by the King at the time of DB. West Knoyle took its alternative form, *Cnoel hodierne*, from a former tenant called *Hodierna*. The 1086 form gives some indication of the inaccuracy of many spellings in the Domesday Book.

Lackham S. of Chippenham
1086 Lacham 1232 Lakham Edw.I Lackam 1430 Lackham

OE *lac-ham*, 'homestead or hamlet by the small stream', referring to a minor tributary of the Bristol Avon. LACOCK has a similar first element.

Lacock S. of Chippenham
854 Lacok 1086 Lacoch, Lacoc 1166 Lachoca c1210 Lacoq 1260 Lacock 1439 Laycock

Probably OE *lac-oc*, the first element being the 'small stream' also found in LACKHAM. The suffix is either adjectival, giving 'streamy place', or diminutive, giving 'streamlet'. Lacock lies on a small tributary of the Bristol Avon. An alternative first element may be OE *leac*, as in LATTON.

Lake S.W. of Amesbury
1289 Lake 1324 Lake

As in LACOCK, this is from OE *lac* or *lacu*, with reference to a former tributary of the Salisbury Avon, now only a dry valley.

Landford E. of Downton
1086 Langeford 1242 Laneford 1295 Landeford

Either *langa-ford*, 'long ford', or *lane-ford*, 'ford where the lane crosses the river'. The second explanation is the more likely as the river here is only a minor branch of the Test. A ford still exists today on the western boundary stream in Giles Lane, to the west of Landford Manor. The 'd' in the present name is evidently a late introduction.

Langford, Little N.W. of Wilton
1211 Parve Langeford c1290 Langeforde pṽa Edw.II Lutlelanggeford 1332 Litelangeford 1428 Parva Langford

Langa-ford, 'long ford', probably with reference to the river crossing at STEEPLE LANGFORD.

Langford, Hanging and **Langford, Steeple**

See HANGING LANGFORD and STEEPLE LANGFORD.

Langley Burrell N.E. of Chippenham
940 ad Langelegh' 1086 Langefel, Langhelei 1181 Langelega 1289 Langleye Burel c1290 de Longaleye 1333 Langle Burel 1535 Longley Burrell

Langan-leah, 'the long clearing or meadow'. The Burrell family held the manor from the time of DB until the early 14th century. Peter *Burel* is recorded as tenant in 1242. The village lies to the south-east of KINGTON LANGLEY.

Larkhill N.W. of Amesbury
1360 Larkehull 1617 Larkehill

Self-explanatory. This modern military settlement takes its name from the hill on which it stands.

Latton N. of Cricklade
1086 Latone 1204 Lacton 1249 Lattetone c1290 de Lattone

Probable OE *lac-tun*, 'farmstead by the stream' — the village lies between the River Churn and the smaller Ampney Brook. Alternatively, the first element may be *leac*, 'leek', or *(ge)lad*, 'canal, way or course' (there is evidence that the course of the Churn was indeed diverted at Latton, probably in Roman times, to supply two local mills). See CRICKLADE, and also LACKHAM.

Laverstock (larstock) E. of Salisbury
1086 Lavertestoche, Lavvrecestohes 1221 Laverkestok 1227 de Laverstoke 1302 Lavirkestok 1310 Larkestok

OE *læwerce-stoc*, 'settlement frequented by larks'. Longstaff claims that the River Bourne, on which Laverstock stands, was referred to as the *Læfer* in an old charter.

Lavington, Market S. of Devizes
1086 Laventone 1242 Stuppellavintona 1254 Stepellavinton 1316 Stapul Lavynton 1397 Chepynglavyngton 1412 Lavyngton Gernon 1460 Lavington Forum 1496 Est Lavyngton 1681 Markett Lavington

Lafinga-tun, 'farmstead of Lafa's people'. As the present name recalls, there was formerly a weekly market here, although, as a royal charter was not granted until 1254, it is unclear whether the 1242 form incorporates OE *stapul*, 'market', or OE *stipel*, 'steeple', referring to the tower of the parish church (towers *were* formerly called steeples). The ME *Chepyng* and Latin *Forum* also denote the market. Roger *Gernon* held the manor in 1242, and also held EASTERTON. 'East' to distinguish from LAVINGTON, WEST, and also to refer to the particular part of the parish in which the church and village lay. With its long market street, Market Lavington is of similar layout to BEDWYN, GREAT.

Lavington, West S. of Devizes
1086 Laventone 1233 Lavinton' Episcopi 1294 Lavynton 1628 West Lavington

See LAVINGTON, MARKET. The Bishop of Sarum was chief tenant here in 1086. Also known until recently as Bishop's Lavington.

Lea S.E. of Malmesbury
1190 Lia 1249 Lya 1268 Legh 1346 la Lee

The primary meaning of OE *lea* or *leah* is 'wood' or 'clearing in a wood'. However, there is often confusion with OE *læs*, 'leaze or meadow', which leads to an alternative interpretation. Place-names incorporating *-leah* are most commonly found in areas of forest, where settlements were founded in natural or man-made clearings. This village lay within the bounds of BRADON Forest.

Leigh S.W. of Westbury

See WESTBURY LEIGH.

Leigh S.W. of Cricklade
1242 Lia   1249 la Leye   1561 Lighe

As with LEA, this village once stood in a clearing of BRADON Forest. Interestingly, both Lea and Leigh incorporate the French article *la* in their early forms.

Leigh Delamere N.W. of Chippenham
1236 Leye   1428 Lygh, Legh   1488 Ligh   Eliz.I Lye Dallamer

See LEA, above. Adam *de la Mere* held the manor in 1236.

Liddington S.E. of Swindon
940 at Lidentune   1086 Ledentone   1156 Lidetona   1242 Ludinton   1279 Lydington   1321 Ludyngton

From OE *hlydan-tun*, 'farmstead on the stream called lyden or loud one'. The stream is still known as the Liden, or Lyden, Brook. For parochial purposes the name is usually spelled Lyddington. For Liddington Hill, see BADBURY.

Limpley Stoke W. of Bradford
1263 Hangyndestok   1333 Stok   1348 Stokewere   1585 Lymply Stoke

From OE *stoc*, 'stockaded place, settlement'. The village is situated at the foot of a steep river-cliff, or *hanging*, and there is a weir here by the Avon Mill. The meaning of Limpley is unknown.

Littlecote N.W. of Hungerford
Littlecott E. of Enford
Littlecott N.E. of Hilmarton

Predictably, these three names are all derived from OE *lytla-cote*, 'small cottage or cottages'. Their individual etymological histories are similar.

Littleton N.E. of Trowbridge
1268 Lytelton   1306 Lyttleton   1470 Litilton

OE *lytla-tun*, 'little farmstead'.

Littleton Drew W. of Grittleton
1065 Litletun   1086 Liteltone   1311 Littleton Dru   1316 Litleton Drewe   1351 Lutlyngton Dru

See LITTLETON, above. The *Druele* and *Drury* families were followers of William the Conqueror. Walter *Driwe* held the manor in 1220. The feudal suffix was possibly added to avoid confusion with the nearby larger settlement of GRITTLETON.

Littleton Pannell (Panell) S. of Devizes
1086 Liteltone   1317 Lutleton Paynel

As LITTLETON, above. This settlement was probably 'little' in comparison with the nearby *tun* of LAVINGTON. *Panell* was a follower of the Conqueror whose descendant, William *Paynel*, held the manor in 1249. There is a Pagnell Lane in the village.

Lockeridge W. of Marlborough
1086 Locherige 1316 de Lokerugge

Possibly *Lucan-hrycg*, 'Luca's ridge', ie. the downland to the south of the river Kennet. The personal name *Lucumon* is recorded in the Anglo-Saxon Chronicle.

Longbridge Deverill
1086 Devrel 1241 Deverelungpunt 1253 in Longs Ponte Deverell 1316 Deverill Langebrigge 1428 Deverell Longepond

See BRIXTON DEVERILL, which lies upstream on the river Wylye. It is impossible to say whether Longbridge has OE origin, as the earliest available forms are in French (*punt*, 'bridge'), which may signify a Norman origin instead. In 1428 English form shows some confusion in translation from the French.

Longford S.E. of Salisbury
956 æt Langanforda 1086 Langeford 1316 Langeford 1485 Langford Cervyngton

Descriptive of a long ford across the Avon, situated near the late 16th century Longford Castle. The 1485 form is of unknown origin.

Longleat W. of Warminster
1235 la Langelete 1281 Longa Leta 1315 Langelete 1333 Longleat 1366 le Langlete herne

Langa-(ge)læt, 'long water channel', referring to the long stream which flows northwards to the Rodden Brook. The river was flooded to form ornamental lakes when Sir John Thynne built his beautiful house here in the late 16th century. The 1366 form includes the OE *hyrne*, 'corner or angle'.

Luckington N.W. of Grittleton
1086 Lochintone 1201 Lokintun 1242 Luckintona 1296 Lokyngtone 1382 Luckington

Lucinga-tun, 'farmstead of Luca's people'. See LOCKERIDGE.

Ludgershall N.E. of Amesbury
1015 Lategaresheale 1086 Litlegarsele 1135 Lotegarsal c1150 Ludkereshala 1166 Lutegareshal 1234 Luttegarishal 1251 Ludgershall 1271 Lotegareshal 1279 Lutlegreshale 1572Lurgassill

The first element is the personal name *Lutegar*. The second element is possibly OE *healh*, 'nook or corner', but more likely is OE *heall*, 'palace or residence', ie. Ludgershall Castle. The present castle ruins date from the 11th century, but it is likely that an earlier fortification stood on the site before the Norman Conquest.

Publish'd 20 Feb.ʸ 1772, by S. Hooper, No. 25 Ludgate hill. R. Godfrey, sculp.

Ludgershall Castle, 1772

Ludwell E. of Shaftesbury
1195 in Ludewell̄ 1252 Ludewele 1341 Lodewulle

Possibly *Ludan-wielle*, 'Luda's well or small stream': the village lies on a short tributary of the Nadder. Or *hlydan-wielle*, 'loud spring or stream'. See LIDDINGTON.

Lediard Tregoze

Lydiard Millicent and **Lydiard Tregoze** (Tregoz) (tregooz) N.E. of Wootton Bassett
900 Lidgeard, Lidegaerd, Lidgerd 1086 Lidiarde, Lediar 1268 Lydyerd Mylisent, Lydyerd Tregos 1283 Northlideyerd 1349 Suth Ledyerd 1473 Luydeyard Mylcent

Possibly this is OE *Lydan-geard*, 'Lyda's girded or enclosed place', referring to a fenced-in part of BRADON Forest. Jones puts forward the Old Welsh word *llidiart*, meaning 'opening, gate or gap', possibly descriptive of an entrance to Bradon Forest, which may have once marked the boundary between Welsh and Saxon tribes. The area was still extensively wooded at DB. Millicent de Clinton was a 12th century owner of the manor of Lydiard Millicent, which was also known as North Lydiard. Lydiard Tregoze, according to John Aubrey, was once known as Lydiard Ewyas or Ewias, from the family that held it after the Conquest (see also TEFFONT EVIAS). In the early 12th century, it passed to the *Tregoz* family, who took their name from a village in the arrondissement of St Lô in northern France. Robert *Traigoz* held the manor in 1242. The property passed to the St John family in the reign of Richard I. See also FIFIELD BAVANT.

Lyneham S.W. of Wootton Bassett
1268 Lynham 1285 Linham 1290 Lynhm̄ 1428 Lynham 1571 Lyneham

OE *lin-ham*, 'homestead where lin or flax was grown'. Longstaff suggests *lind-ham*, 'homestead by the lime-trees'. The lime was probably once the dominant tree in much of lowland Britain. In the Domesday Survey, Lyneham was assessed as part of BRADENSTOKE.

Maddington W. of Amesbury
1086 Wintreburne 1178 Maydenewynterburna 1198 Medinton 1230 Maidingtuna 1277 Madintun 1314 Wynterbourn Maydeneton 1428 Madyngton

The original name was *Wintreburne*, from the local stream: see BERWICK ST JAMES and WINTERBOURNE STOKE, which lie downstream. Possibly the present name is OE *Madinga-tun*, 'farmstead of Mæd's or Mada's people', although a likely alternative is 'maiden's *tun*', named after a local holding of the nuns of Amesbury. See also MAIDEN BRADLEY.

MAIDEN BRADLEY, S.W.
Wiltshire.

Maiden Bradley N. of Mere
1086 Bradelie 1178 Deuerell Puellarum, Deverell Puellarum 1210 Bradele Hen.III. Suht Bradeleigh 1228 Bradleigh Leprosi 1267 Meydenebradele 1271 Maiden Bradley 1281 Deverill c1290 Bradele Abbis

Originally OE *braden-leah*, 'wide clearing or meadow'. The village is situated at the source of the river Deverill, for the derivation of which name see BRIXTON DEVERILL. An ornate drinking-fountain and water-trough dated 1891 stands in Church Street, and bears the following inscription:–

> Drink, travellers, drink of Bradley's purest rill,
> Which, strange to say, runs quite a mile up hill;

There was a priory one mile to the north, and a small cell of nuns ('maidens') belonging to Amesbury was founded as a hospital for *leprous maidens* in the 12th century. *Puellarum* is Latin 'of, or belonging to, the young women'. See also MADDINGTON. The 1178 form is a mis-spelling of South Bradley, and distinguishes this village from BRADLEY, NORTH.

Malmsbury Crofs. Wilts.

Malmesbury
675 Maldumesburg 681 Meldunesburg 701 Maldumes buruh 705 Maildulfi urbs 745 Malduneuse monasterium 758 in Maldubiensi monasterio c770 Maldubia civitate 854 Malmesburg 934 Meldulfuensis Burgi c1050 Maldmesbyrig 1086 Malmesberie 1201 Maumesbir 1252 Maumesbiri

A plethora of early spellings. The second element is OE *byrig*, '*burh* or fortified place', which is an apt description of Malmesbury's position. Leland writes that " the toune of Malmesbyri stondith on the very toppe of a greate slaty rok, and ys wonderfully defendid by nature". The first element is a personal name: according to William of Malmesbury, the name is *Maildulf*, Black Prince and Scottish founder of the monastery. Other authorities favour *Meldum* or *Malmud*, a 5th century king, as the founder of the original fortress here. The modern name is due largely to confusion with Bishop Aldhelm (died 709), the Malmesbury abbot who erected a monument and chapel on the site of Maildulf's cell in 642. A wide variety of names are found on coins minted at Malmesbury. *Urbs* is Latin for 'town'; *civitate* is Latin for 'community or settlement'. Malmesbury stands on the Bristol Avon, formerly called *Ingelbourne*, 'Ingeld's stream', and a late 7th century reference to *Ingelbourne-castel* probably describes the fortress, which the Britons in earlier years knew as *Caer Bladon* (cf. BROKENBOROUGH). Malmesbury was made one of the 9th century Saxon *burhs*, or defensive posts, by King Alfred: others in Wiltshire were sited at CHISBURY, CRICKLADE and WILTON.

Manningford Abbots, Bohune and **Bruce** (manniford) (boon) S.W. of Pewsey
987 Maningaforda 1086 Maneforde, Maniford 1200 Manegesford 1275

Parva Maningford, Maningford Petri 1279 Manyngeford Bon, Manyngeford Breuse 1289 Manyngford Abbatis 1290 Manningeford Ab̃bis Edw.I Maningford Parva 1428 Manyngeford Abbatis, Manyngford Sancti Petri

OE *Maninga-ford*, 'the ford of Mana's people'. Referred to as *Merce ford* in a Saxon charter, the original river crossing was probably adjacent to the mill in Manningford Bruce, on the old trackway to Manningford Abbots. A former estate of the Abbey of St Peter, Winchester, Manningford Abbots was also known as Manningford Parva or Little Manningford. John *de Boun*, a relation of the Bohun earls of Hereford, was resident at Manningford Bohune in 1263: this village's former name of Manningford St Peter comes either from the Abbey of St Peter, or Herbert *filius Petri* ('Fitzpeter'), who held lands here in 1242. The village church, too, is dedicated to St Peter. William *de Breuse* inherited the manor of Manningford Bruce in 1275. The first Domesday entry refers to Manningford Abbots, the second to the other two villages.

Manton W. of Marlborough
1086 Manetune 1229 Maniton' 1265 Manniton 1289 Manynton

'Mana's *tun* or farmstead', possibly with reference to the same person whose name occurs in MANNINGFORD. Longstaff puts forward the Celtic word *maen*, 'stone', for the first element, descriptive of the greywether stones which are found in the Manton area.

Marden S.E. of Devizes
940 on mærdenum 941 Mercdene 963 Merh daene 1086 Meresdene 1170 Mercdena 1211 Mereden 1280 Mereghedene 1359 Hyrgheden

The second element is OE *denu*, 'valley'. The first is either *mearh*, 'horse', or *mære*, 'boundary'. As the River Avon flows past the village in a shallow valley which also forms the parish boundary between Marden and Beechingstoke, the most likely meaning is 'boundary valley'.

Market Lavington

See LAVINGTON, MARKET.

Marlborough
c1072 Mærlebi 1091 Marleberge c1150 æt Mærle beorg 1140 Mællesberiense Castellum 1148 Merleberga 1175 Melleberga 1229 Marlborough 1361 de Merleborowe 1428 Marleburg 1485 Marborowe

Traditionally believed to be derived from *Moerla-beorh*, 'Moerlin's barrow or burial place'. The prehistoric artificial mound which formed the nucleus of Marlborough Castle is reputed to be the burial place of the Irish magician, the mysterious Merlin. In support of this theory, the motto on the Borough Arms reads *Ubi nunc sapientis ossa Merlini* — 'Where now are the bones of wise Merlin'. Alternative first elements which ought to be considered are OE *mærlic*, 'noble or lofty'; *marl*, with reference to the chalk marl soil here; and even the composite *mære-leah*, 'boundary meadow'. The earliest form of the name appears on a silver penny minted at Marlborough during the reign of William I.

B. St Peters. *View of Lord* Hartfords House *at* Marlborough 29 *Iun.* 1723. A. *the Scite of the Roman Castrum*

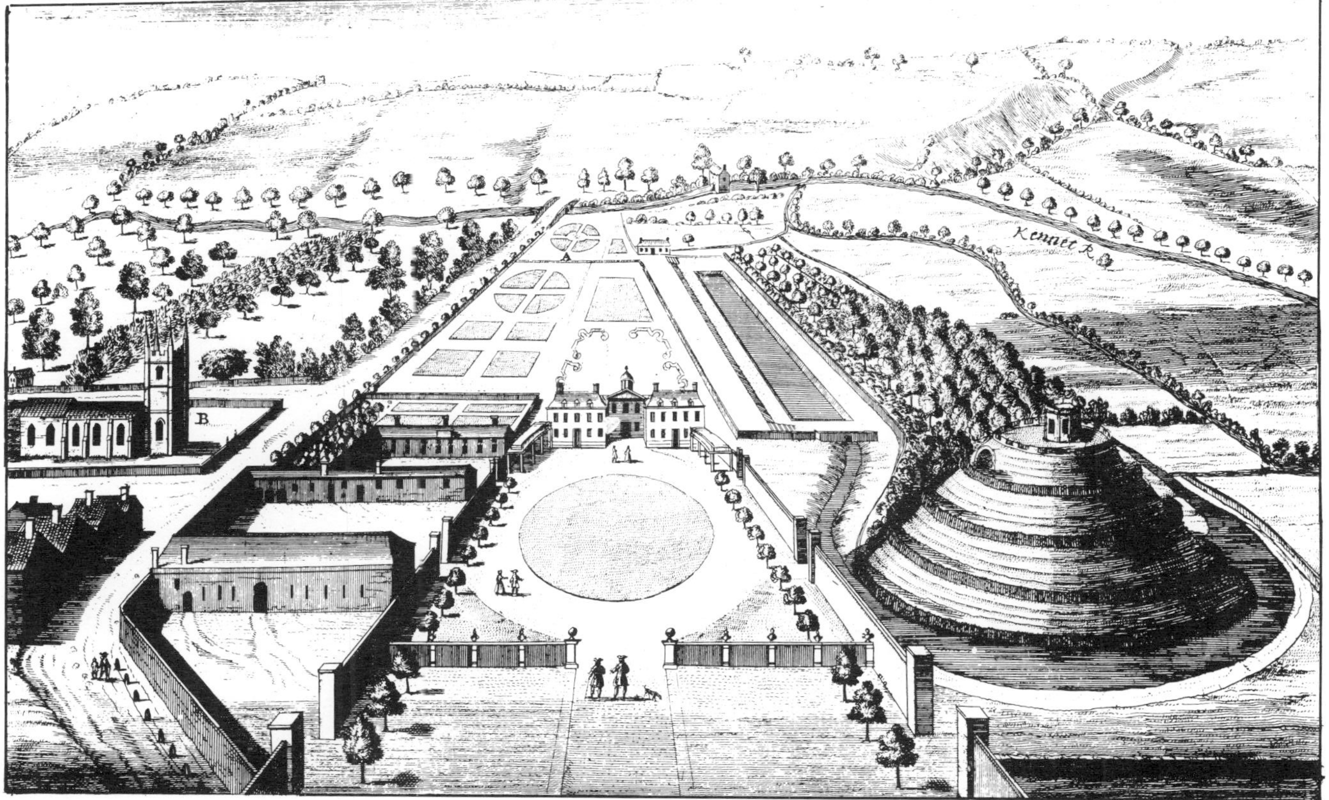

Stukeley del:

Marston S.W. of Devizes
1289 Mershton 1309 in Merstone 1428 Merssheton

OE *mersc-tun*, 'farmstead by the marsh'. The village lies on low ground near a tributary of the Semington Brook. Another possible interpretation of the name is *mære-stan*, 'boundary stone'. As Richard Jefferies remarked in Chapter 3 of "The Amateur Poacher", marshes often formed boundaries, so either meaning of the first element makes sense.

Marston Meysey N.E. of Cricklade
1281 Northmerston 1301 of Mershtone Meysi 1316 de Northe Mershton

See MARSTON, above. The village is situated on low land near the Thames. Roger *de Meysi* held the manor in 1211. The name Meysey has striking similarity to EYSEY (meaning 'low-lying land near the Thames') and, apart from the initial 'M', may have a similar derivation. 'North' to distinguish from MARSTON, SOUTH. Also spelt Marston Maisey during the last century.

Marston, South N.E. of Swindon
1198 Merston 1262 Merston 1330 Suthmershton 1392 Meryshton 1553 Southemaston

See MARSTON, above. 'South' to distinguish from MARSTON MEYSEY. The author Alfred Williams, who lived in the village, interpreted the name as *merestane*, or 'mark-stone', noting that South Marston was "commonly called *Maaston*".

Marten S.W. of Hungerford
1086 in Mertone, Martone 1200 Mereton 1278 Marthon

OE *mære-tun*, 'farmstead at the boundary', possibly referring to the parish boundary with Grafton or a border marked by the Mildenhall-Winchester Roman road.

Melksham
1086 Melchesham 1155 Melkesham 1229 de Milkesham' 1281 Mulkesham

Probably from ME *melche-ham*, 'milk-settlement or homestead', a name which would have been used to describe a dairy-farm. Alternative first elements include OE *milisc*, *melisc*, 'muddy or wet meadow', or an early form of the name Michael, to whom the parish church is dedicated.

Membury N.E. of Ramsbury
c1090 Minbiry 1196 Mimbyre 1263 Mimmebir' 1289 Membir'

Probably *min-byrig*, '*burh* or fort on the brink or border' (*min* derives from the Cornish language). Membury Fort, a vast, overgrown Iron Age defensive structure dating from c75 BC, straddles the Wiltshire/Berkshire boundary.

Mere
1086 Mera, Mere 1281 Meyre 1316 Mayre 1308 Meere

OE *(ge)mære*, 'boundary or landmark'. See also MARSTON. Mere probably grew up as a Saxon frontier settlement near the boundaries of Wiltshire, Somerset and Dorset. *Mere* remained in use until the last century as a dialect word for a boundary line, often in the form of a ditch or a bank of turf.

Midgehall N. of Wootton Bassett
1165 Mighal' 1268 Michehale 1319 of Miggehale 1571 Mudgehall

Micgan-heall or *Micgan-healh*, 'Micga's hall or corner of land'. Or possibly the name is *mycg-healh*, 'corner of land frequented by midges'.

Mildenhall (mynall) E. of Marlborough
803/5 Mildanhald 1086 Mildenhalle 1241 in Mildehale 1428 Myldenhale

Mildan-heall, 'Mildred's hall' (or *-healh*, as in MIDGEHALL). The Roman settlement of *Cunetione* or *Cunetzione* was at Black Field, Mildenhall. At the meeting-place of five Roman roads, this important 1st century fort and town, of which no trace now remains, took its name from *Cunetio*, the Celtic term for the river Kennet. See KENNETT, EAST and WEST.

Milford E. of Salisbury
1086 Meleford 1236 Muleford 1280 Mileford 1354 Mulleford Richard

OE *mylen-ford*, 'ford by the mill'. Richard *filius Petri* ('Fitzpeter') held the manor in 1198.

Milston N. of Amesbury
1086 Mildestone 1178 Mildistona 1203 Midleston 1330 Mulleston

Mildan-tun, 'Mildred's farmstead' (see MILDENHALL). On the assumption that the 1203 form is accurate, Ekwall puts forward OE *midlesta-tun*, 'mid-most farmstead'. The 'u' in the 1330 spelling represents a secondary 'y'.

Milton Lilbourne (liburn) E. of Pewsey
1086 Mideltone 1198 Middelton 1249 Mydilton Lellebon 1281 Middelton Lillebon 1412 Milton Lilborn 1416 Milton

Originally *middel-tun*, 'middle farmstead', probably because the village lies midway between Pewsey and Easton Royal. William *de Lilebone*, whose ancestors came from Lillebonne in northern France, held the manor in 1236: see also FIFIELD BAVANT.

Minety N.E. of Malmesbury
844 Minty, Mintih, Mintig 1156 Minti 1232 Menthi 1247 Munte 1428 Mynty 1552 Mynetye

OE *minte-ieg*, 'marshy land where the water-mint grows'. Aubrey wrote, ". . . at Mintie is an abundance of wild mint". The earliest spellings suggest a different pronounciation from that of today. The 1232 form seems to be an attempt to translate the original English name into French (*menthe*, 'mint').

Monkton Deverill N.E. of Mere
1086 Devrel 1189 Munketon 1275 Deverel Monketon 1340 Monkendeverel 1525 Est Monketon

Upstream from BRIXTON DEVERILL. The Abbot of Glastonbury was tenant of the manor at DB and there was also a pre-Conquest Benedictine monastery here. Hence: 'monk's farm'. The former prefix, 'East', describes the village's position in relation to KINGSTON DEVERILL. Also known as Over Deverill because of its position upstream.

Monkton Farleigh N. of Bradford
1001 at Farnleghe 1086 Ferleia 1228 Broctun Parva 1316 Farley Monachorum 1364 Munkes Farlegh 1400 Monken Farlegh

OE *fearn-leah*, 'fern or bracken clearing'. A Cluniac priory dedicated to St Mary Magdalene was founded here in 1125. Also known as *Broctun Parva* or Little Broughton prior to the 14th century, in comparison to the larger village of BROUGHTON GIFFORD.

Murcott N. of Malmesbury
1065 Morcotun 1202 Morcote

Mor-cote, 'cottages by the moor or wasteland'. The 1065 form incorporates the suffix *-tun*.

Netheravon S. of Enford
1086 Nigravre, Nigra avra 1115 Netheravon 1158 Nederavena 1211 Niterehavene 1226 Nutheravene 1290 de Nytherhavene

Nither-afene, literally 'lower or further down the Avon', describing Netheravon's position in relation to UPAVON.

Netherhampton (netherington) S. of Wilton
1209 Otherhampton 1242 Notherhampton 1316 Nether Hampton 1333 Nitherhampton c1570 Netheryngton

Nither-ham-tun, 'the lower farmstead', perhaps because it is south of the River Nadder in relation to QUIDHAMPTON. Also to distinguish from CHILHAMPTON and DITCHAMPTON.

Nettleton W. of Grittleton
940 at Netelintone 1086 Niteletone 1186 Netlinton 1189 Netelinctona 1242 Netelton 1428 Netylton

Nyttelinga-tun, 'the farmstead of the people of Nytta'.

Newnton, North S.W. of Pewsey
892 North niwetune 934 Nywantune 1086 Neweton 1212 Newentone 1222 Neyton 1290 Northnyweton 1571 Newington

New farmstead. 'North' in contrast to NEWTON, SOUTH. The present spelling retains the dative 'n' of the original Saxon form.

Newton, South N. of Wilton
943 Sud Niwetune, niwantune c1190 Nyweton 1242 Sutneuton 1290 de Suthnywetone 1453 Sowthe Newton

New farm. 'South' to distinguish from NEWNTON, NORTH.

Newton Tony or **Toney** E. of Amesbury
1086 Newentone 1268 Newynton 1270 Niwetona (Umfridi de Bohun), Niwetone (Johannis de Nevill) 1332 Nyweton Tony 1363 Newynton Tony

New farmstead. Ralph *de Toenye* held the manor in 1254, a descendant of the Norman family who took their name from the French village of Tosny, near Rouen. The 1270 forms indicate local landowners.

Norrington W. of Broad Chalke
1198 Norkington 1211 Northamtona 1227 Northinton 1307 Northynton 1361 Northynkton

OE *Northinga-tun*, denoting a farmstead belonging to the tribe of a man called Northman or Northgar. Alternatively, the present name may be a corruption of *north-ham-tun*, 'north farmstead', brought about by local dialect in the same way as BECKHAMPTON is sometimes pronounced 'Beckington'.

Norton S.W. of Malmesbury
931 Northun, Northon, de Nortone 1086 Nortone 1281 Northton

North-tun, 'north farmstead', perhaps in relation to Hullavington.

Norton Bavant N.W. of Heytesbury
1086 Nortone 1242 Northton 1335 Norton Scydemor 1381 Nortonbavent 1428 Norton Bavent

'North farmstead', in relation to Sutton Veny which lies one mile to the south. Alesia *de Bavent* held the manor in 1293, taking her name from the village of Bavent, near Caen in France: see FIFIELD BAVANT. Geoffery *de Escudemor*', who held the manor in 1242, was a member of the same family that held UPTON SCUDAMORE.

Oaksey N.E. of Malmesbury
1086 Wochesie c1180 Wogasca 1197 Wokesia, Wokeseye 1299 Wockesygh 1428 Wokesey 1452 Woxey 1535 Okyssey 1585 Oxey

OE *Wocces-ieg*, 'Woc's marshy or well-watered land'. The village stands on low ground between the Swill and Flagham Brooks. The original pronounciation of 'Wokesy' remained in currency until the last century.

Oare N. of Pewsey
934 oran, Motenesora 1229 in Ore 1428 in Oare 1440 Oure 1585 Woore

From the OE word *ora*, descriptive of the border or edge of a hill, in this case Huish Hill or Oare Hill, which rise steeply to the north of the village. *Motenesora* evidently incorporates an OE personal name.

Odstock S. of Salisbury
1086 Odestoche 1173 Odestokka 1199 Odestoka 1242 Oddestok 1428 Odestok

Odan-stoc, probably 'Oda's settlement or stockaded place'.

Ogbourne Maizey, Ogbourne St Andrew and **Ogbourne St George** N. of Marlborough
946/55 Oceburnan 1086 Ocheburne, Ocheborne 1133 Occheburna c1143 Ocheburna magna et parva 1208 Okeburn 1242 Ockeburn' Meysy 1268 Okeborne Prioris 1277 Hokeburn Edw.I Northokeburne 1291 Okeburn Major, Okeburn Minor 1316 Okkeburne Parva, Okkeburne Magna 1390 Auquebourne majori

Occan-burna, 'Ocea's stream': the name *Ocea* is recorded in several 9th century charters. The stream on which the villages stand, a tributary of the Kennet, is now called the Og, ie. it is a back-formation from the original place-name. An alternative first element is OE *ac*, 'oak'. Ogbourne Magna and North Ogbourne were former names for Ogbourne St George, which was also the site of a small priory, founded by Maud of Wallingford c1149. Ogbourne Maizey, the hamlet in the parish of Ogbourne St Andrew, was held by Robert *de Meysy* in 1242: see also MARSTON MEYSEY. St George and St Andrew are the respective church dedications. The 1309 form shows considerable French influence.

Old Sarum

See SALISBURY.

Old Dilton

See DILTON MARSH.

Orcheston St. Mary, 1836

Orcheston St George and **Orcheston St Mary** N.W. of Amesbury
1086 Orchestone, Orcestone 1195 de Orchesden 1227 Orkeston 1279 Orcheston Seynt Jorge 1281 Horcheston 1291 Orcheston Boyvile 1315 Ordrycheston 1404 Orcheston Marie 1428 Orcheston Georgii, Orcheston Boyvile

OE *Ordrices-tun*, 'Ordric's farmstead', a similar personal name to that found in URCHFONT. The suffixes refer to church dedications. Henry *de Bovile* held the manor of Orcheston St Mary in 1242.

Overton, East W. of Marlborough
939 Oferan tunes land 1086 Ovretone 1167 Ouerton Prioris 1316 Overton Fifide 1682 East Overton

A former tithing of OVERTON, WEST, adjacent to the parish of FYFIELD. Formerly a possession of the Abbey of St Swithin's, Winchester.

Overton, West W. of Marlborough
939 Uferan tune 949 aet Ofærtune 972 æt Uuertune 1263 Uverton Abbisse 1275 Westovertone 1284 Overton 1316 Overton (Abbatisse)

OE *uferan-tun*, 'the upper, or over, farmstead', perhaps in respect of the village's position near the source of the Kennet. Longstaff suggests *ofer-tun*, 'farm on the river-bank or shore'. The Abbess of Wilton was tenant here from 1066 until the Dissolution. See OVERTON, EAST.

Oxenwood S.W. of Hungerford
1265 Oxinwood 1332 Oxenewode

'Oak-wood' or 'oxen-wood'. Formerly within the boundaries of CHUTE Forest.

Patney S.E. of Devizes
963 æt Peatanige, to Peattanige, to Pittanige c1050 æt Peattaniggi 1171 Pateneye 1230 Pateneia 1243 Pattenei 1284 Patney

Peattan-ieg, 'Peatta's island or well-watered land'. The River Avon divides above the village and re-unites below it, effectively forming an islet at the southern end of the former Cannings Marsh (see ALL CANNINGS). Or the first element may be 'peat'.

Paxcroft E. of Trowbridge
1249 Packelescrofte 1281 Pachelescrofte 1574 Paxcroft

Probably 'Pæccel's croft or small enclosed field'.

Pertwood N.W. of Hindon
1086 Perteworde 1166 Ptewurda 1270 Purtewerthe 1324 Perteworth 1535 Pertewodde

This name is made up of an unknown personal name combined with OE *weorth*, 'farmstead', which has since been corrupted into '-wood'.

Pewsey
c880 æt Pefesigge, Pevesy, Pefesy 940 Pevesige 1086 Pevesie 1166 Peuesia 1261 Peveseye c1290 Peveseya 1378 Pusye 1428 de Peueseye

Pefes-ieg, 'Pefe's marshy or well-watered land'. The name *Pefe* is of Celtic origin. Pewsey stands near the source of the Salisbury Avon.

Pewsham S.E. of Chippenham
1238 Peusham 1263 Peusham 1284 Pewesham 1303 Pevesham 1320 Powesham 1448 Peuisham

Probably *Pefes-ham* or *Peufe's ham*, 'Pefe's homestead': see PEWSEY. The earlier forms refer to Pewsham Forest, which before the 14th century was also known as the Forest of Melksham and Chippenham. Pewsham is on the Cocklemore Brook, formerly called the Pewe (*1279 aque de Pewe*).

Pickwick N. of Corsham
1268 Pykewyk 1279 Pycwyk

Probably a combination of OE *pic*, 'sharp point' and *wic* 'dairy farm'. Upper Pickwick is on a well-marked spur of land.

Pitton E. of Salisbury
1165 Putenton' 1198 Putton 1273 Puttone c1300 Piton 1402 Putton

Pytt-tun, 'pit farmstead', or *Puttan-tun*, 'Putta's farmstead'. The personal name *Putta* derives from the OE word for a hawk. If the first interpretation is correct, the pit in question was probably a small quarry in the chalk of the escarpment cliff to the east of the village.

Porton S.E. of Amesbury
1086 in Poertone, Portone 1160 Pourton 1199 Portun' 1211 Powertone 1281 Pouerton 1428 Porton

The village stands on the Port Way, the Roman road from Old Sarum to Silchester. The name is possibly derived from an original 'farmstead on the Port Way'. It has been suggested that the first element comes from an old name for the River Bourne.

Potterne S. of Devizes
1086 Poterne 1146 Poternam 1195 Poterna 1316 Potterne 1585 Pottren

Potterne possibly incorporates the same Saxon personal name as is found in PITTON. Hence: 'Putta's dwelling' (*Puttan-ærn*). 'Dwelling where pots are made' is an alternative meaning. CHITTERNE, COLERNE and VASTERNE also have second elements derived from *-ærn*.

Poulshot S.W. of Devizes
1086 Paveshou 1187 Paulesholt 1242 Pawelseholt 1322 Paulesholtes 1331 Palesholt 1422 Polesholt

Paules-holt, 'Paul's wood or copse': see HOLT. The straggling nature of Poulshot, with its common to the north, is characteristic of a woodland village. John Aubrey paints a grim picture of Poulshot, labelling it a "wett dirty place" with its inhabitants "appearing in the spring time of primrose complexion"! At first sight the DB entry, *Paveshou*, appears hopelessly inaccurate, although the 'v' probably represents a 'u' — these two letters were virtually interchangeable in the 11th century alphabet.

Preshute W. of Marlborough
1185 Prestcheta 1249 Presteshethe 1252 Preschut 1313 de Purshute 1332 Preshute 1385 Pershuyt 1426 Presshuyte 1530 Presshett

The meaning of the first element is unknown. The second element is either the Celtic word *ceto*, 'woodland', as in CHUTE, or OE *ciete*, 'cottage or cell belonging to a priest', possibly with reference to the small priory which existed at nearby CLATFORD.

Purton Church and Manor

Purton N.W. of Swindon
796 Piertean, Puritone, Perytun 854 at Peritune 1065 Piritune 1086 Piritone 1281 Pyryton 1327 Puryngton 1375 Piryton Keynes 1494 Pereton

The root of this name is the OE word *pirige*, 'pear tree', and the early form *Piertean* means simply 'at the pear-tree' rather than 'pear-tree farm' which the other forms suggest. John *Keynys* held the manor in 1428: see ASHTON KEYNES.

Purton Stoke N.W. of Swindon
1086 Stoche 1476 Puryton Stoke

Originally *æt stoce*, 'the stockaded place or settlement'. Attached to the manor of Purton.

Quemerford S.E. of Calne
1199 Quemerford 1227 Kemerford Hen.III. Quembreforde 1240/5 Quemerford 1293 Quimerford 1476 Comerford

The second element is obviously *ford*, but the first is less obvious. As Quemerford stands at the confluence of two headwaters of the river Avon, it is possible to consider the Welsh *cymmer*, 'confluence'. Longstaff calls it 'Cynemere's ford', stating that it is the supposed site of a battle recorded in the Anglo-Saxon Chronicle.

Quidhampton (quidington) W. of Salisbury
1249 Quedhampton 1289 Quidhamton 1324 Quidhamptone 1331 Quedehampton 1459 Quyddehampton

Possibly OE *cwead-ham-tun*, literally 'dirt or dung homestead'. *Quid* or *queed* is also an old Wiltshire dialect word, meaning 'cud', derived from the OE word *cwidu*. See also CHILHAMPTON.

Rabson N. of Avebury
1086 Wintreborne 1178 North Wynterburn 1199 Noȓt Wintborñ 1242 Abbedeston 1275 Rabbedestone 1279 Rabboteston 1316 Rabbesdeston 1544 Robston 1588 Northwynterborne al. Rabeston

For an explanation of the DB entry, see WINTERBOURNE BASSETT and BERWICK ST JAMES. Rabson is probably OE *Radbodes-tun*, 'Radbod's farmstead'. The 1242 form either shows confusion with the original name, or is indicative of an alternative derivation, ie. ME *at ther Abbedeston*, since corrupted to *Rabbedeston* by the transfer of the 'r' from the definite article to the name itself. If *Abbedeston* is accurate, the meaning is thus *abbodes-tun*, 'abbot's farmstead' (Rabson was held by the Abbess of Amesbury at DB).

Ramsbury
909 (ad ecclesiam) Corviniensem 947 Rammesburi c990 Hremnesbyrig c1050 Reamnesbyrig 1023 Coruiniensis (ecclesiæ) 1086 Ramesberie 1091 Rammesbiri 1146 Rammesberiam 1227 Remmisbiri 1232 Remesbir' 1275 Ramsbury

OE *hræfnes-byrig*, 'the raven's *burh* or fortified place'. The symbolism of 'raven' is unclear, although it probably represents a personal name. Some early forms incorporate the Latin *corvus, corvi*, 'raven', and *ecclesia*, 'church'. The Latin termination *-ensis* was often applied to ecclesiastical settlements (see also MALMESBURY). Ramsbury was the seat of the ancient Bishopric of Wiltshire, created by the West Saxons in 909.

Ratfyn N. of Amesbury
1086 Rotefelde 1115 Rotefen 1178 Rocefen 1270 Rothefen 1428 Roffen 1560 Rothfenne

Probably *Hrothan-fenn*, 'Hrotha's fen or marsh'. The village is on low land by the Salisbury Avon.

Redlynch S.E. of Salisbury
1282 Radelynch 1470 Radeling 1567 Redlynche

Read-hlinc, 'the red ridge or rising ground', or *Radan-lynch*, 'Rada's lynch or ploughed hillside'. The village is on high ground to the east of the Salisbury Avon.

Ridge E. of Hindon
1407 Rugge 1558 Ridge

OE *hrycg*, 'ridge of the down, or ridgeway'. Stands on the prominent Ridge Hill.

Rockley N.W. of Marlborough
1086 in Rochelie 1155 Rokeleya 1222 Rokel 1234 la Rokele 1270 Roclea 1301 Roukley 1335 Rookle 1428 Rokele 1591 Templerookley

Hroc-leah, 'clearing or meadow frequented by rooks'. Or the meaning may be 'rocky meadow', with reference to the greywether stones which litter the dry valleys in this part of the Marlborough Downs. The 1591 form refers to Temple Farm, to the north-west, where the Knights Templars held lands from 1155.

Rodbourne S. of Malmesbury
701 Reodburna 758 Rotburne 844 Rodburne 1065 Rodburna 1232 Redburn 1289 Rudburne 1453 Roddeborne

OE *hreod-burna*, 'reedy stream', referring to an affluent of the Bristol Avon.

Rodbourne Cheney (cheeny) N. of Swindon
943 on hreodburnan 1086 Redborne 1291 Rodeburn 1304 Rodburne Chanu 1410 Rodebourne

See RODBOURNE, above. This *burn* is a tributary of the river Ray, and the earliest form refers to the stream itself rather than the settlement on its banks. The name *Cheine* is of Norman origin. Ralph *le Chanu* held the manor in 1242.

Rollestone W. of Amesbury
1086 Wintreburne 1242 de Rolvestone 1325 Wynterburne Rolveston 1428 Rolveston

The present name appears to be a post-Saxon *tun*-formation, with the possible meaning of 'Ralph's farmstead'. For *Wintreburne*, see WINTERBOURNE BASSETT and BERWICK ST JAMES.

Rood Ashton S.E. of Trowbridge
1307 Chapel Ashton 1474 Rode Assheton 1596 Rowde Asheton

See STEEPLE ASHTON. The prefix is OE *rod*, 'cross', perhaps denoting a wayside cross or place where people would gather in the open for worship. Longstaff writes that "A monastery (some say a chapel) was founded at this place, so it is said". The manor was formerly held by Romsey Abbey. A reference to *rodestan*, within the boundaries of Ashton, is made in a Saxon charter, and possibly describes an early stone cross here.

Roundway N. of Devizes
1149 Rindweiam 1262 Rindway 1332 Ryndewey 1337 Ryndway 1493 Rundewey

Hringan-weg, 'Hringa's road or way', or *rymed-weg* 'cleared road'. Roundaway was a local variation of the name.

Rowde N.W. of Devizes
1086 Rode 1186 Rudes 1196 Rodes 1287 Roudes 1428 Rowes

Rowde is of uncertain origin. Two possibilities are OE *hreod*, as in RODBOURNE, or OE *rod*, as in ROOD ASHTON.

Rushall (russall) S.W. of Pewsey
1086 Rusteselve, Rusteselle 1160 Rusteshala c1200 de Rusteshale 1281 Rosteshale 1285 Rusteshell 1397 Rusthalle 1535 Russall

Rustes-heall or *-healh*, 'Rust's hall or nook of land'. The parish boundaries form a ¼ mile-wide neck of land to the south-west of the village, which may be the 'nook' in question.

J. Ryland del. et sculp.

The North East View of Salisbury.

Salisbury (saulsbury)
4th c. Sorviodunum, Sorbiodonum 552 æt Searo byrg, Searo byrig, Sælesberi 1003 to Searbyrig 1086 Sarisberie 1091 Sarum 1125 of Særesbyrig 1132 of Seresberi 1146 Sarisberiaæ 1195 Veteris Sarum 1205 Salesbir̃ 1218 Veteres Sarisbirias 1227 Novæ Sarum (Sarisberiæ) 1268 Saresbyriam 1319 Old Sarum 1336 Salesbirs 1428 Nova Sarisburia c1540 Old-Saresbyry

The forms prior to 1195 refer exclusively to the former city at the Iron Age fortress site of Old Sarum, which in its lifetime has been occupied by a succession of peoples: Celts, Romans, Saxons, Danes and Normans. From about 1200 the new (Latin *nova*) city of Salisbury is distinguished from the

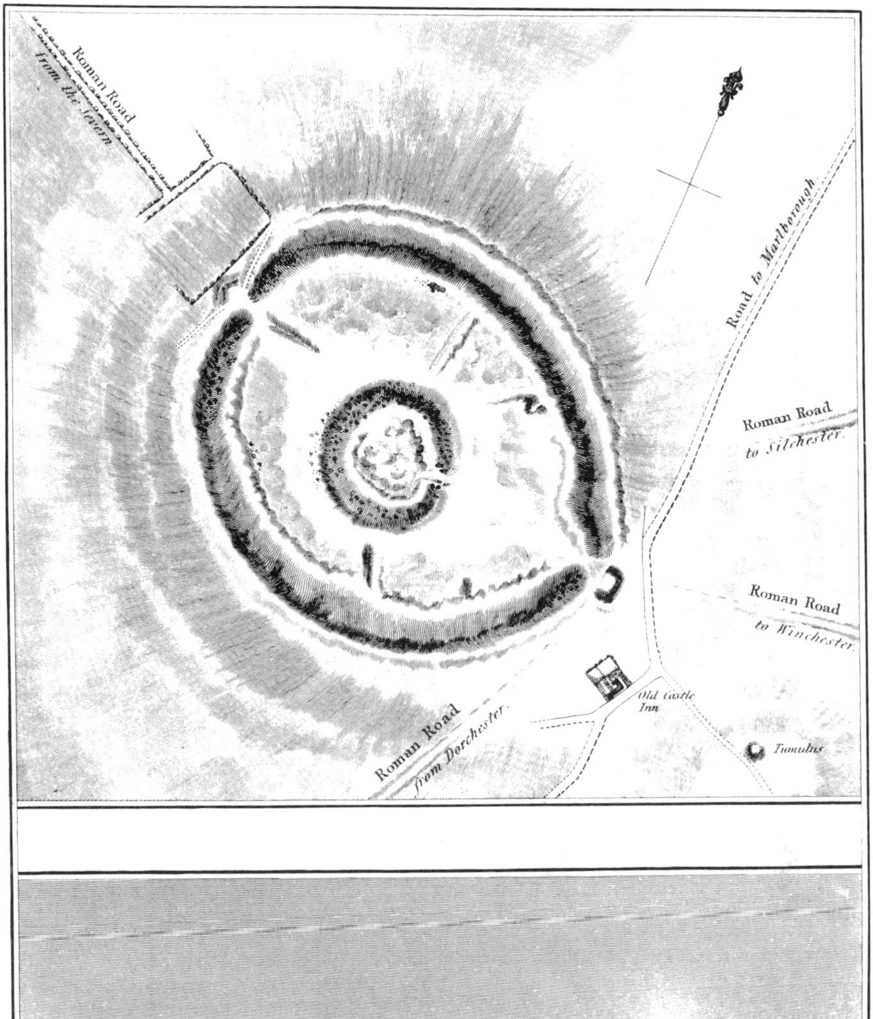
Roman Road
Road to Marlborough
Roman Road
to Silchester
Roman Road
to Winchester
Old Castle
Inn
Roman Road
from Dorchester
Tumulus

Old Sarum

old (Latin *veteris*) fortress, which gradually diminished in importance during the 13th century with the construction of a new cathedral at the riverside site to the south of Old Sarum. The earlier 4th century references come from the Antonine Itinerary, compiled during the Roman occupation of Britain. *Sorbiodonum* may be translated as 'Sorbio fort', although the meaning of the first element is obscure. Later Saxon renderings of the name corrupt the first element to *Searo-*. The original second element was the Celtic word *dun*, 'hill fortress', later substituted by OE *byrig*, which has identical meaning. Today's name of Salisbury has come about by the evolution of the first element from *Searo-* to *Saris-* and finally *Salis-*, this last form being adopted by the Normans during the 12th century. Thus the name is unusual in that it has a Celtic root with an English suffix. Sarum is an artificial name formed from the first element of *Sarisberie* with the Latin termination *-um*. The 12th century Welsh name for the city was *Caer Garadog*.

Salterton N. of Salisbury
1199 Saltertun 1289 Saltreton 1309 Saltertone, Salterton Derneford 1332 Salterne 1428 Salterton 1641 Psalterton

Originally *sealtera-tun*, 'farmstead of the salt-workers or dealers in salt'. *Derneford* refers to the neighbouring village of DURNFORD. The 1641 form is interestingly archaic.

Salthrop S.E. of Wootton Bassett
1086 Salteharpe 1198 Sauteharp 1241 de Saltharp' 1351 Saltharpesway 1428 Saltharp 1455 Salthorp

Probably OE *sealt-thorp*, denoting a place where salt was stored for sale. Significantly, the OE term *sealt-hearpe* signified a salt-sifter. *Saltharpesweye* was an ancient trackway leading northwards from Avebury, through Salthrop, Lydiard and Cricklade, to Cirencester.

Sandridge N.W. of Devizes
1268 Sandrug' 1281 Sandregge 1418 Sandrigge

Sandridge lies on the same Lower Greensand ridge as the nearby villages of SANDY LANE and SEEND.

Sandy Lane S.W. of Calne

A modern name of obvious origin. See SANDRIDGE.

Savernake Forest (savernak) S.E. of Marlborough
934 Safernoc (silva) 1222 de Savernak 1224 Severnak 1232 Savernak 1248 Savernac 1426 Savernack

The medieval Forest of Savernake formerly linked up with the Forest of CHUTE on the Wiltshire/Hampshire border. Possibly the name is connected with a root identical to that in the name of the River Severn (Irish *sabhrann*, 'boundary'), with the Celtic suffix *-aco*. Ekwall suggests a derivation from an old name for a local stream, possibly the BEDWYN.

Seagry S. of Malmesbury
1086 Segrie c1220 Segreya 1224 Segrey 1242 Secre 1249 Segre 1258 Segree 1318 Oversegree 1399 Segreth 1420 Over Segreve 1428 Segre 1773 Over Seagry, Nether Seagry

Possibly OE *secg-rith*, 'sedge stream', or *Sigaran-ieg*, 'Sigar's island or low-lying land'. *Sigar* is the name of a recorded Saxon landowner. Over and Nether Seagry are today's Upper and Lower villages.

Sedgehill S.W. of Hindon
Hen.I Segilla 1289 Seggehull 1439 Segill 1493 Seggehill

OE *secg-hyll*, 'hill where the sedge grows'. The name is given to the district here, which even on the higher ground has many pools and streams.

Seend (seen) W. of Devizes
1190 Sinda 1194 Seinde 1203 Sendes 1211 Sende 1283 Scheynde 1316 de Sende 1650 Sceene

Undoubtedly this is derived from OE *sænde*, 'sand', which may be interpreted in this case as 'sandy place'. Seend stands on the top of an isolated sand hill, an outlier of the Lower Greensand outcrop, upon which SANDRIDGE and SANDY LANE also stand.

Selwood
9th c. Sealwudu c1000 Selewudu 1228 Selewod

The Forest of Selwood once formed an almost impenetrable barrier of woodland between Wiltshire and Somerset, stretching for over 15 miles along the western boundary lands of the county. The name is OE *sealh-wudu*, 'sallow or withy wood', although the Celts knew it as *Coit Mawr*, meaning 'great wood'.

Semington N.E. of Trowbridge
1249 Semelton 1289 Semneton 1300 Semelynton 1470 Semington

Possibly *Seminga-tun*, 'farmstead of Sema's folk'. Or the name may be 'farmstead on the Semnet', with reference to the pre-English name for Semington Brook.

Semley N.E. of Shaftesbury
955 on Semeleage c1190 Semele 1225 Semlegh

The 955 form seems to refer to the river Sem, which rises at Sem Head in the centre of the parish and flows eastwards towards the Nadder. A charter dated 984 describes the river as the *Semene*, although the name is of unknown derivation. OE *Sem-leah* is thus 'clearing or meadow by the river Sem'.

Sevenhampton (sennington) S. of Highworth
Hen.III Sevehampton 1262 Sevenhampton 13th c. Suvenhantone 1330 Senhampton 1608 Sennington

Literally 'the seven homesteads' or 'the enclosure of the seven home-farms', indicating that the original name was perhaps the plural, *Sevenhamptons*. Sevenhampton in Gloucestershire is also pronounced 'Sennington' (see also SEVINGTON). The village is two miles south-east of HAMPTON.

Sevington N.W. of Chippenham
1043 æt Seofonhæmtune 1086 Sevamentone 1289 Sovenehampton 1512 Sevyvyngton

See SEVENHAMPTON, which although of similar derivation has assumed a less abbreviated modern spelling. According to Jones, Sevington was the original name of Grittleton parish.

Shalbourne S. of Hungerford
955 Scealdeburnan 1086 Scaldeburne, Saldeborne 1198 Scaldiburne 1242 Scaudebrne 1329 Westshaldebourne 1375 Chaldebourne 1494 Shalburne 1540 Chauburne

Scealdan-burna, 'shallow stream', referring to an affluent of the Kennet which rises west of the village.

Shaw N.W. of Melksham
1166 Schaga 1199 in Saghe 1256 Schawe 1370 Chaw 1428 in Shawe 1641 Shaa

OE *sceaga*, 'shaw or copse', describes a tract of woodland which in early medieval times was a remnant of the Forest of Selwood.

Sherrington S.E. of Heytesbury
968 Scearntune 1086 Scarentone 1130/5 Serenton 1248 Sernton 1282 Schernton 1300 Scharnton 1316 Sharenton 1324 Schrynton 1348 Sharrenton 1375 Charnton 1413 Sherrington

Scearn-tun, 'mud or dung farmstead'.

Sherston (shaaston) W. of Malmesbury
896 Scorranstan 1016 æt Sceorstane 1086 Sorstain, Sorestone 1167 Scorestan 1215 Sarestan' 1236 Shorestan 1237 Schorestan 1280 Sherston Magna 1316 Sherston 1335 Sharston, Magna Charston 1428 Sherston

Probably OE *sceard-stan*, 'boundary stone', indicating a border between two territories. Sherston stands near the Wiltshire/Gloucestershire boundary and the former dividing-line between the Saxon kingdoms of Wessex and Mercia. *Sceard* is often corrupted by local dialect to 'Shore' and explains the form of the present name. Once known as Sherston Magna to distinguish from SHERSTON PARVA.

Sherston Parva W. of Malmesbury
1242 Parva Scorstan' 1316 Sherston Parva 1351 Sherston Pinkeneye

A smaller village than nearby SHERSTON. Also known as Pinkney, after Ralph *de Pinkenny*, who held lands here in 1201.

Stukley delin. Toms sculp.

A prospect of Silbury hill *from the spring head of the Kennet River. 13. May. 1724.*

Shrewton W. of Amesbury
1086 Wintreburne 1232 Winterbourne Syreveton 1255 Schyrreveton Edw.I in Schreveton' c1290 Schirreneston 1302 Wyntreburn Shirveton 1310 Sherritone 1348 Shirreston 1428 Shereveton

OE *Scirgerefan-tun*, 'sherriff's farmstead', probably with reference to the owner of the manor at DB. The 11th century name of *Wintreburne*, 'winter-stream', was also applied to neighbouring ELSTON, MADDINGTON and ROLLESTONE, which all stand on the infant river Till. See BERWICK ST JAMES and WINTERBOURNE BASSETT.

Silbury Hill W. of Marlborough
c1235 Selleboruwe 1281 Seleburgh 1540 Selbyri, Selburi hille 1663 Selbury, Silbury

Although Silbury was probably a site of Bronze Age ritual significance rather than a burial mound, the name is nevertheless derived from OE *sele-beorg*, 'harvet hill or barrow', indicating that Silbury's original function had been forgotten by the time its present name was first applied. The first element recurs in the name of the former Selkley Hundred (*1196 Selkele; 1291 Sulkele*), whose courts possibly met on the top of Silbury Hill. Aubrey, writing in the 17th century, recounts the legend that ". . . the hill was raysed while a posset of milke was seething".

Slaughterford N.W. of Corsham
1176 Slachtoneford 1186 Sclachtesford 1291 Slahteford, Slahtereford 1299 Slaghtenford 1303 Slaghterford 1343 Slaughtreford 1428 Slaghtreford

Camden takes the name at face value, claiming that here was the ford on the By Brook where the Danish forces were slaughtered by the Saxons during the 9th century campaigns. Another possibility is OE *slah-thorn-ford*, 'ford where the sloe-thorns grow'. However, judging by the 12th century form, *Slachtoneford*, the second element could well be OE *tun*, 'farmstead'.

Somerford, Great and **Little** S.E. of Malmesbury
683 Sumerford 956 somerford 1065 Sumerford 1086 Sumreford 1252 Somerford Maudut 1268 Sumerford Mautravers 1409 Brode Somerford 1428 Somerford Magna, Somerford Parva

The name indicates that the Avon here was fordable only during the summer months, probably at the spot where Park Lane crosses the river at the northern edge of Great Somerford. Longstaff quotes a writer in the Wiltshire Archaeological Magazine as saying that there was no bridge here "until quite recent times". Great Somerford, otherwise 'Broad' from OE *brad*, was held by Walter *Maltravers* in 1196. Little Somerford was held by John *Mauduth* in 1275.

Sopworth W. of Malmesbury
1086 Sopeworde 1201 Sopewrth 1252 Shopwurth Edw.I de Suppeworth' 1298 de Soppeworthe 1428 Soppeworth

OE *Soppan-weorth*, 'Soppa's farmstead'.

Southwick S.W. of Trowbridge
1196 Sudwich' 1249 Suthwik Hen.III Southwick 1322 Sothewyke 1539 Sowthick

Suth-wic, 'southern grange or outlying dairy-farm', attached to Trowbridge. For *wic*, see also BERWICK BASSETT.

Standen N.E. of Ludgershall
778 in standene 1086 Standene, Standone 1249 Standen 1275 Northstanden' 1289 Suthstaunden 1300 Grenestaunden 1316 Staunden Chaworthe 1327 Staundene

Stan-denu, 'stony valley', describing the small dry valley below Chute Causeway in which Standen lies. There are sarsens here. Hugh de Standene held the manor in 1242 from Patricius *de Chaurces*, whose surname is corrupted to *Chaworthe* in the 1316 form. The meaning of *Grenestaunden* is unknown.

Standlynch S.W. of Salisbury
1086 Staninges 1198 Stanlinc' 1249 Stanlinghe Edw.I Stanling' 1361 Stallynch 1388 Stanlynch 1398 North Stanlynch 1403 Stanlynch

Stan-hlinc, 'stony ridge or ploughed hillside'. This former medieval settlement lies near REDLYNCH. On the dubious assumption that the DB entry is more reliable than the 1198 form, there is a possibility that the name is a tribal one, with a personal name for the first element, as in ALL CANNINGS.

Stanton Fitzwarren S.W. of Highworth
1086 Stantone 1299 Staunton 1312 Staunton juxta Hegheworth 1327 Stontone 1362 Bychenstoke Staunton 1392 Staunton Fitzherberd 1394 Staunton Fitz Waryn 1555 Staunton Fitz Brynde

OE *stan-tun*, 'enclosure fenced in by stones'. or 'farmstead by the stone': apparently a large standing-stone once stood here. Fulco *filius Warini* held the manor in 1196; Herbertus *filius Johannis* in 1319; and Thomas *Brynde* of Wanborough in 1554. The Latin word *filius* is equivalent to the old French prefix *fitz*, which means 'son of'. For *Bychenstoke*, see BEECHINGSTOKE.

Stanton St Bernard E. of Devizes
903 Stantun 957 Stantune 1086 Stantone 1275 Stauntone 1402 Staunton Fits Herbard 1553 Staunton Barnarde

See STANTON FITZWARREN, which seems to have had an identical name to this village at the end of the 14th century, ie. *Staunton Fits Herbard. Berners* was a follower of the Conqueror, while *Erebertus* is recorded as holder of the manor in 1242. See also ALTON BARNES. Also known as Stanton Abbess, after the Abbey of Wilton, once a major landowner in the parish.

Stanton St Quintin N. of Chippenham
1086 Stantone 1286 Stanton St Quintin c1290 Staunton 1317 Staunton Quyntyn 1428 Staunton (Sancti Quintini)

See STANTON FITZWARREN. Herbert *de Sancto Quintino* held the manor in

1211, a descendant of the Norman family of St Quentin, who originated from the town of the same name in northern France. See also FIFIELD BAVANT.

Stapleford N. of Wilton
1086 Stapleford *1115 Stapelford* *1428 Stapulford*

Stapul-ford, 'ford marked by a post or staple', which would probably serve to indicate the shallowest place in the stream. Stapleford is on the River Till near its confluence with the Wylye. For alternative first elements, see STEEPLE ASHTON.

Staverton N. of Trowbridge
1086 Stavretone *1212 Staverton* *1509 Stafferton* *c1540 Stavertun*

OE *stæfer-tun*, 'enclosure marked by poles or stakes', or *stoefera-tun*, 'scribe's farmstead'. Longstaff suggests that the name is a corruption of *stan-ford-tun*, 'farm by the stony ford': the village lies on the main Bath road by the Bristol Avon.

Steeple Ashton E. of Trowbridge
880/5 æt Æsctune, de Ascketune *964 Æystone, Aystone* *1086 Aistone* *1268 Stepelaston, Chirchaston* *Edw.III Stepell Asschton* *c1290 de Hastone, Astone* *1391 Stipelasshtoun* *1485 Stepul Aisshon*

The original name was simply Ashton, ie. *æscan-tun*, 'ash-tree farmstead', a description which also encompassed the neighbouring lands of ASHTON, WEST and ROOD ASHTON. The prefix is probably OE *stipel*, with reference to the former 15th century steeple on the parish church of St Mary. John Leland, the 16th century antiquarian, wrote that "the spired steeple of stone is very fayre and high". Sadly it was struck down by lightning in July 1670. However, the alternative interpretation of OE *stapul*, 'market' should not be ruled out, as a weekly market was granted by Henry III in 1266, and a stone market cross (OE *stapol*) still stands in the village. Longstaff claims that the village was also called Market Ashton.

Steeple Langford N.W. of Wilton
943 æt langanforda *1086 Langeford* *c1290 Langeford Magna* *1294 Stepel Langeford, Stupellangeford* *1316 Steppul Langford* *1331 Stapel Langford*

Descriptive of a long ford across the river Wylye. Although the parish church has a tower, the meaning of OE *stipel*, 'steeple', should not be ruled out: see STEEPLE ASHTON and LAVINGTON, MARKET. Formerly known as Great Langford in contrast to LANGFORD, LITTLE and HANGING LANGFORD.

Stert S.E. of Devizes
1086 Sterte *1189 Stoerte* *1196 Stuerte* *1283 Storte* *1311 Steurte* *1333 Sturt* *1402 in Steerte* *1428 in Sterte*

OE *steort*, 'projecting tail or point of land'. An apt description, as Stert stands upon a prominent spur which forms the watershed between the two river Avons.

Stitchcombe E. of Marlborough
1086 Stotecome 1200 Stutescombe 1275 Studescombe 1282 Stotescombe 1316 Stutescumb 1574 Stichcombe

OE *Stutan-cumb*, 'Stut's valley', with reference either to the Kennet valley or a smaller dry valley behind Coombe Farm.

Stockley S. of Calne
1281 Stokele 1319 Stoclygh 1327 Stockeleye 1445 Stockley

Stocca-leah, 'meadow or clearing with stumps of felled trees'. Formerly within the old Forest of Selwood.

Stockton S.E. of Heytesbury
1086 Stottune 1166 Stoctun' 1284 Stocton c1290 de Stottone 1316 Stokton

Assuming that the DB is inaccurate, this is OE *stoc-tun*, 'enclosure fenced in with stocks or posts'.

Stoford N. of Wilton
943 Stanford 1196 Staneford 1242 Stafford 1285 Stoford 1352 Stouford 1453 Stofford 1466 Stoweford 1559 Stovorde

OE *stan-ford*, 'stony ford'. The river-crossing was probably across the Wylye to the neighbouring village of Great Wishford. See also STOWFORD, which has a similar meaning.

Stoke Farthing E. of Broad Chalke
955 be eastan stoke, to stoc hæmalande 1258 Stokes 1273 Stok 1289 Stoke Verdon 1316 de Stoke 1428 in Stoke Verdon 1570 Stoke Verthing

Originally OE *stoc*, which has the approximate meaning of 'settlement or stockaded place' (see BAVERSTOCK). 'Farthing' is a corruption of the French name Verdun. John *de Verdun* held the manor in 1258, taking his surname from the family home in north-east France: see also FIFIELD BAVANT. The earlier forms without the feudal suffix refer to what is now Stoke Farm. *stoc hæmalande* may be interpreted as 'the land belonging to the dwellers at Stoke'.

Stonehenge W. of Amesbury
c1130 Stanhenges, Stanenges c1250 Stonheng

From OE *stan-hencga*, 'hanging stones', with reference to the lintels of the outer stone circle which literally 'hang' in the air. The modern word 'henge' originates from the nomenclature of Stonehenge, and is now widely used to describe any prehistoric stone monument. Although the Neolithic structure of Stonehenge dates from about 2800 BC, the earliest available written references are as late as the 12th century, over 3000 years after its conception.

Stonehenge

Stourton N.W. of Mere
1086 Stortone 1182 Sturtoñ 1279 Storton 1302 Steortone 1315 Stourtone 1332 Stourton c1540 Stourtoun

Stour-tun, 'farmstead by the river Stour' (*944 Sture; 968 Stoure*), the name of which is probably derived from a Celtic word meaning 'strong, powerful'. The river rises nearby, to the north-west of Stourhead, site of the stately home built in 1722 by Colin Campbell. Leland wrote that "the ryver of Stoure riseth there of 6 fountaines or springs".

Stowell, East and **West** N.W. of Pewsey
1176 Stawelle 1300 Stowelle 1327 Eststowelle 1392 Weststouwelle

Probably OE *stow-wielle*, 'dwelling-house by the spring or stream'. Or the first element may be *stan*, in which case the name describes a spring or stream marked by stones. East Stowell, deserted since the early part of the last century, lay near Wilcot.

Stowford S.W. of Bradford
987 stanford 1199 Stafford 1327 Stovord 1458 Stowford

See STOFORD, which is of similar derivation.

Stratford-sub-Castle N.W. of Salisbury
1091 Stratford 1316 de Stratforde 1397 Stratford subtus castrum Veteris Sarum 1485 Stratford (-under-the-Castle-of-Old-Sarum)

OE *stræt-ford*, 'ford on the Roman way or street'. Two Roman roads crossed the Avon here: the road from Old Sarum to the Mendip Hills, and the Port Way, running south-west towards Dorchester. Stratford, as the Latinised name suggests, lies at the foot of Old Sarum hill. The present name dates from the 19th century and is an adaptation of the 14th century Latin version.

Stratford Tony S.W. of Salisbury
672 on stretford 948 on streat ford 986 Strétford 1086 Stradford 1275 Strateford 1316 de Stratforde 1332 Stratford Tony, Stratford Touny

See STRATFORD-SUB-CASTLE. The Port Way crossed the River Ebble just to the west of the present village. Ralph *de Touny* held the manor in 1242, and also the manor of NEWTON TONY.

Stratton St Margaret or **Lower Stratton** and **Stratton, Upper** N.E. of Swindon
1086 Stratone 1240 Overe Stratton 1281 Muchelestratton, Nutherestratton 1316 Stratton Inferior, Stratton Superior 1427 Stretton sanct' Margaret' 1630 St Margarett Stratton al. Nethetowne al. Throppe

OE *stræt-tun*, 'farmstead on the Roman road', ie. Ermin Street, which linked the Roman settlements of Cirencester and Speen. The suffix 'St Margaret' refers to the dedication of the parish church which, in turn, may have been named after Queen Margaret, who held Stratton in dower in 1316. Upper (Latin *Superior*) Stratton stands on slightly higher ground than Lower (Latin *Inferior*) Stratton, the nucleus of which was formerly known locally as The Street. *Nuthere* is from OE *nither*, which also means 'lower'; *muchele* is from OE *michel*, 'great', referring to the larger village of Upper Stratton. *Throppe* is of unknown origin.

Studley W. of Calne
1175 Stodlega 1194 Stodleia 1249 Stodlegh

Stod-leah, 'stud meadow or clearing', describing a place where a stud of horses was kept.

Sutton Benger N. of Chippenham
854 at Suttune, at Suthtune 1054 Sudtone 1086 Sudtone c1290 Suttone 1377 Sudetone Berenger 1488 Benger 1497 Sutton Leonard

OE *suth-tun*, 'southerly farmstead', perhaps in relation to Hullavington. *Berenger* was a French family name, and the DB records that *Berengerius* (Latinised form) held the manor in the 11th century. The origin of the 1497 name is unknown.

Sutton Mandeville S.E. of Hindon
1086 Sudtone 1275 Sutton (Maundevyle) 1535 Sutton Maundvild

South farmstead, in relation to Chilmark or Teffont. Robert *de Mandeville* held the manor in 1224.

Sutton Veny S.W. of Heytesbury
1086 Sutone, in Sudtone 1225 Magna Sutton 1268 Fennisutton 1297 Fenne Sutton 1298 Great Sutton 1341 Fenny-sutton 1365 Litel Sutton 1535 Veny Sutton

South farmstead, in relation to NORTON BAVANT. The suffix is either a French family name or descriptive of the village's marshy situation, ie. 'in the fens'. The two villages of Great and Little Sutton were in existence by the mid-13th century. Great (or Magna) Sutton is the present village.

Swallowcliff or **Swallowcliffe** S.E. of Hindon
940 Swealewanclif 1086 Svaloclive 1115 Swaleweclive 1276 Swalfklyfe, Swaluweclive 1288/92 in Sualwecliffe 1339 Swalclyff 1428 in Swaluclyve, de Swaluclyffe 1618 Swakley

OE *swealewe-clif*, 'hill or cliff frequented by swallows'. The village stands at the head of a steep coombe beneath the scarp of Swallowcliffe Down. For the second element, see also CLEVANCY.

Swindon
1086 Suindone, Svindune 1156 Swindona 1205 de Swinedoñ 1247 Theveneswyndon 1252 Swindon 1275 Nether, Alta Swindon' 1289 Chepyng Swyndon 1302 Hauteswyndon 1324 Swyndon Valence, Heghe Swyndon 1386 Hiswyndon 1493 Thevyn Swyndon

OE *swina-dun*, 'hill where pigs are kept'. Alternatively the first element may be the personal name *Sweyn*, the 11th century Danish king, who possibly held Swindon when on his way to capture Bath in the campaigns of 1013. William *de Valence* held the manor in 1252. *Chepyng* comes from OE *ceap*, referring to the market which was held here from the 13th century, although a charter was not granted until 1616. High (Latin *Alta*) Swindon is the hill-top site of the original market town, now known locally as Old Town. Nether and Even Swindon were respectively the lower and flatter pasture lands to the north of the parish.

Teffont Evias and **Teffont Magna** (teffunt) W. of Wilton
860 be Tefunte 940 Teofuntinga gemære 964 at Teofunten 1086 Tefonte Hen.III Theofunta 1236 Tifhunt 1242 Hewyas Tefunte 1268 Over Tefunte 1275 Teffunt Ewyas 1335 Teffonte Ewyas 1418 Teffount Hungerford 1493 Over Teffent 1584 Upperteffont

Either *teo-funta*, 'boundary spring or stream', or *Teowan-funta*, 'Teowald's spring or stream'. A clear, fast-running affluent of the Nadder rises in a chalk-pit beside the road to the north of Teffont Magna and runs for a mile southwards through the main street of both villages. Jones suggests that *Teff* was a former name for this stream. OE *funta* is an all-purpose word, which may also be used to describe a fountain or well. Teffont Evias (also known as Teffont Ewyas until the 19th century) belonged to the barons of Ewyas Harold, a village in Herefordshire, during the 13th century. The DB entry refers to Teffont Evias, which later was also known as Teffont Hungerford, after Walter Hungerford, who held property here. Teffont

Magna, the larger village, was otherwise referred to as Over Teffont because of its position upstream. The 940 form means 'the boundary of the people of Teffont' and describes the parish bounds between Teffont and Wylye.

Thickwood W. of Chippenham
1086 Ticoode 13th c. Thikwude 1289 Thikkewode c1460 Thikwode 1540 Thychewood

Descriptive of a dense wood. The valley sides on the Avon/Wiltshire border are still thickly wooded.

Throope S.E. of Salisbury
1289 Thrope 1327 Throp, Thorp 1332 Throup 1428 Le Throp

OE *thrope*, 'dependent settlement'. This is probably the place referred to in 1289 as *Ebblesburnthorpe*, ie. 'the settlement dependent on EBBESBOURNE WAKE'.

Tidcombe N.E. of Ludgershall
1086 Titicome 1197 Titecumbe 1230/40 Tydecomb 1249 Tydecumbe 1282 Tytecumbe Husee 1298 of Tytecumbe 1339 Tidecombe Huse

OE *Tidan-cumb* or *Titan-cumb*, 'the small valley belonging to Tida or Tita'. The manor was held in 1282 by Hubert *Husee*: see TIDWORTH.

Tidworth (tedworth) S.W. of Ludgershall
10th c. Tudanwyrthe 1086 Todeworde, Todowrde 1178 Thudewrda Johannis Marescalli, Thudewrda Hogonis de Lucy 1211 Todeworthe 1227 Tudeuurth 1270 Tudeworda 1278 Northtudewrthe 1300 Todeworth Husee 1313 Northtodeworth 1324 Todeworth Melewys 1428 Tudeworth

OE *Tudan-weorth*, 'Tuda's farmstead'. The 13th and 14th century feudal suffixes all indicate local landowners, and Matthew *Husee* is recorded as having a holding here in 1242 (see also TIDCOMBE). North Tidworth refers to that part of the village which lies in Wiltshire, while South Tidworth and Tidworth House are across the county boundary in Hampshire. Also spelled Tedworth during the 19th century.

Tilshead (tilzed) on Salisbury Plain
1086 Theodulveside, in Tidulfhide 1167 Tidolfeshida 1238 Tidelveshid 1246 Teovelsia 1390 Tydolside 1394 Tydelsyde, de Tydolveshyde 1397 Tileshed 1421 Tileshide 1492 in Tydelvessyde 1502 Tyleshed 1578 Tylsehed

OE *Theodwulfes-hid*, 'Theodwulf's hide of land'. Tilshead formerly stood at the head of the river Till, but the valley across the Plain is now usually dry until Orcheston, 2 miles south-east. The river-name is a back-formation from the original village name.

Tinhead N.E. of Westbury
1190 Tunheada 1242 Tynhide 1250 Tinehid 1256 de Tenhyde 1280 de Teenhide 1563 Tynehead

This appear to be WS *tien-hida*, 'settlement consisting of ten hides'. See FIFIELD.

Tisbury S.E. of Hindon
759 Tissebiri c800 Tyssesburg, Dyssesburg c915 to Tyssebyrig 984 æt Tissebiri 1086 Tisseberie 1316 Tyssebury 1332 Tisbury 1428 Tissebury

OE *Tissan-byrig*, 'Tissa's *burh* or fortified place', although the personal name *Tissa* does not appear in any local records.

Tockenham S.W. of Wootton Bassett
775/7 Toccansceaga 854 Tockenham 1086 Tocheham 1202 Thokenham c1290 Tokh̄m 1297 Est Tokkenham 1316 Tokkenham 1332 Westockenham 1348 Tokynham

OE *Toccan-ham*, 'Tocca's hamlet or homestead'. The earliest form refers to East Tockenham, now Tockenham Court, while West Tockenham is the present village of Tockenham.

Tollard Royal S.E. of Shaftesbury
1086 Tollard 1166 Tollard 1227 Toulard 1316 de Tollarde 1535 Tollard Ryall

Probably *Tolan-eard*, 'Tola's home or property'. At the time of Edward the Confessor, the manor was held by *Toli*, a descendant of the original owner. King John held a knight's fee at Tollard, and used it as a hunting-seat for the northern parts of Cranborne Chase.

Trowbridge
1086 Straburg 1184 Trobrigge 1211 Troubrigḡ 1250 de Trewbrigge 1316 Trowbrygge 1322 of Troubrigge 1358 de Troughbrigge 1489 Throughbrygge

Probably OE *treow-brycg*, 'bridge made of trees or wood'. Trowle Bridge was situated ½ mile west towards Bradford: see TROWLE COMMON. The DB form appears inaccurate, unless it indicates an alternative derivation.

Trowle Common N.W. of Trowbridge
1086 in Trole 1242 Trulle, Trolle 1479 Trell 1504 Bradfordestrull 1611 Great Trowle

The original site of *Trole* is lost. The name itself may be an alternative term for the Bristol Avon, or there may be some connection with TROWBRIDGE

Tytherington S.W. of Heytesbury
1086 Tedrintone, Tedelintone c1140 Tyderinton c1290 Tuderyngton 1428 Tyderyngton

Tidheringa-tun, 'the farmstead of Tiedre's people', the personal name probably coming from an OE word meaning 'fragile or weak'.

Tytherton, East and **Tytherton, West** or **Tytherton Lucas** N.E. of Chippenham
1086 Terintone, Tedelintone 1196 Tidrinton 1289 Tuderyngton Kaylewey 1327 Tuderyngtone Calowen 1428 Tuderyngton Lucas 1721 Tytherton Lucas al. West Tytherton

This is an abbreviated version of the name TYTHERINGTON which has a similar etymological history. Adam *Lucas* and Elyas *de Kaylewey* were landholders here at the time of Henry III. The hamlet of KELLAWAYS is nearby.

Uffcot S. of Swindon
1086 Ufecot, Ulfecote 1158 Huffecote 1297 Offecote

Probably 'Uffa's or Ulfe's cottages'.

Ugford N. of Wilton
956 Ucganford 1045 Uggafordinga landscore 1086 Ocheforde, Ogeforde c1190 Uggeford Sancti Johannis 1227 Uggeford 1275 Hugeford 1327 Ugeford St James 1428 Ogeford 1544 Northugford, Southugforde, Ugforde Abbesse

Uggan-ford, 'Ugga's river-crossing'. The village, formerly a holding of the Abbess of Wilton, lies by the river Nadder. Its former church was dedicated to St James. The 1045 form is taken from a land charter and refers to 'the boundary of the people of Ugford'.

Upavon (oopaven) S.W. of Pewsey
1086 of Oppavrene 1172 Upeavena 1202 Huphavene, de Uppawne 1240 de Up Aven' 1268 Uppehavene

Originally OE *æt up-Afne*, 'settlement further up the River Avon', describing Upavon's position near the head of the Avon valley in contrast to NETHERAVON, downstream.

Uppington N. of Wilton
1407 Uphampton 1411 Uppington 1599 Uphampton

Probably the present name is a corruption of OE *up-ham-tun*, 'upper homestead' (see also SEVINGTON, which is similarly corrupted), so-called because the village is upstream from Stapleford on the River Till. The alternative is *uppan-tun*, 'high-lying farmstead'.

Upton W. of Hindon
1284 Upton 1289 Upton'

Up-tun, 'upper farmstead', formerly the home of Stephen *de Upton*. This is probably the place referred to in 1202 as *Childecnoel*, ie. 'the settlement dependent on Knoyle': Upton is within the parish of KNOYLE, EAST.

Upton Lovell S.E. of Heytesbury
957 æt Ubban tune, Ubbantun, Ubbantuninga gemære 1086 Uptone 1199 Ubeton 1242 Obeton 1476 Ubbedon Lovell 1526 Lovells Upton

OE *Ubban-tun*, 'Ubba's enclosure or farmstead'. The third 957 form refers to 'the boundary of the people of *Ubbantun*'. William *Lovell* held the manor in 1428.

Upton Scudamore N. of Warminster
c990 æt Uptune 1086 Opetone, Uptone 1221 de Obetuñ 1275 Upton Squydemor 1281 Uptone Escudemor' 1335 Upton Scydemor 1439 Skydemorysupton

The village lies on the western edge of Salisbury Plain, its name meaning 'high or upper farmstead' (OE *up-tun*). The name 'Scudamore' derives from the French family name *Escudamour*. Walter *Skydemore* was the lord of Upton during Stephen's reign in the 12th century, and it was his descendant, Alice, who married Adam Bavent in the late 13th century (see FIFIELD BAVANT and NORTON BAVANT).

Urchfont (ushent) S.E. of Devizes
1086 Jerchesfonte (or possibly *Ierchesfonte*) *1175 Erchesfont, Erkesfonte 1179 de Archesfunte 1242 de Urichesfunte 1259 de Orchesfunte Edw.I Urcheffont 1377 Lerchesfonte 1428 de Orcheffunte 1564 Archfounte al. Urshent*

Eardrices-funt, 'Eardric's spring or fountain', referring to the river source in Urchfont Bottom, to the south-east of the church, which apparently has never been known to fail. The 1377 form incorporates the French article *l'*.

Vastern (Vasterne) S.W. of Wootton Bassett
1229 Fetstern 1235 Fosterne 1267 la Fasterne Edw.I de Wasturne 1300 la Vasterne

Probably OE *Fæstan-ærn*, denoting a dwelling belonging to someone such as *Fæstred* or *Fæstwulf*, both of which are recorded personal names (see also CHITTERNE). Or OE *fæstaern*, 'fast dwelling or stronghold', referring to the fortified manor house. The earliest forms are corrupt.

Wadswick S.W. of Corsham
c1200 Wadeswica 1288 Waddiswyke 1310 Waddeswyk 1623 Wadsick

Wæddes-wic, 'Waedda's outlying farm or dairy'.

Wanborough E. of Swindon
854 æt Wenbeorgan, Wenbergh 1086 Wemberge 1091 Wamberga 1194 de Wenƀge 1196 Wenbergh 1245 Wamberge 1285 Wanberg 1310 Wanbrogh 1325 Whanburgh 1334 Westwambergh 1349 Wamberwe 1365 Estwambergh 1428 Wamburgh

Possibly OE *wenn-beorg*, 'wen-like barrow', with reference to a nearby group of burial mounds on Sugar Hill. More likely the name is a corruption of *Wodnes-beorg*, 'Woden's barrow'. *Wodnesbeorge* is listed in the Anglo-Saxon Chronicle as the site of a great battle between the Saxons and the Britons in 592: authorities place this either at Wanborough or Adam's Grave near Pewsey. Lower and Upper Wanborough were formerly East and West Wanborough respectively.

Wansdyke
903 wodnes dic   936 wondesdich   Hen.III Wodenesdick   1499 Wannysdiche

Woden's ditch or dyke. It was common practice in the Middle Ages to ascribe the origin of mysteries to deities or supernatural beings, eg. Devil's Den, Grim's Ditch. This great Dark Ages frontier earthwork was built by the Romano-British people to stop the Saxon onrush, and although it dates only from the sixth century, the present name would suggest that its original purpose had been forgotten by the 10th century.

Wardour S.W. of Tisbury
899/925 æt Weard oran   1086 in Werdore   1201 Waredovre   1316 de Werdure   1428 in Wardore

OE *weard-ora*, literally 'watch-bank', referring to a Saxon lookout station on the banks of the river Nadder. The second element is also found in OARE.

Warminster
899/925 Worgemynster   1086 Guerminstre   1115 Weminister   1157 Wermenistra   1222 Weremenstr.   1324 in Weremystre   1448 Warmestre

Assuming that the two earliest versions are inaccurate, this is probably OE *were-mynster*, 'monastery by the Were', referring to Swan River which flows into the Wylye. The rebuilt 14th century minster of St Denys replaced an older Saxon structure which had rule over a large area of Wiltshire. Ekwall suggests that the river-name comes from the OE *worian*, 'to wander', although it may be of Celtic origin.

Water Eaton E. of Cricklade
1086 Etone   1281 Nunyeton   1332 Eton Monial'   1372 Watereton   1428 Eton   1726 West Eaton

OE *ea-tun*, 'farmstead by the water', ie. the river Thames. The prefix distinguishes the village from nearby CASTLE EATON. Formerly a holding of the Abbess of Godstow at Oxford, Leland refers to it in the 16th century as *Nunne-Eiton*.

Wedhampton S.E. of Devizes
1289 Weydhampton   1341 Woedhampton   1349 Wedhampton

Probably OE *weod-ham-tun*, 'weed-grown homestead'. Longstaff says that the name was also spelt Quidhampton, but he is probably confusing it with QUIDHAMPTON.

West Ashton

See ASHTON, WEST.

Westbrook N.E. of Melksham
Hen.II in Westbroch   1266 de Westebroke'

OE *west-broc*, 'west brook' or 'place west of the brook', referring to an affluent of the Bristol Avon.

Westbury
1086 Westberie, Wesberie 1115 Westbiri 1227 Westbire 1229 Westbury 1518 Westbury under the playne

If the Domesday Survey is to be trusted, the name is OE *west-berie*, 'westerly open field'. Alternatively, the origin may be *west-byrig*, 'westerly *burh* or earthwork', probably with reference to Bratton Castle, which is the nearest fortification of any significance. The town lies towards the western edge of the county, with Salisbury Plain rising to the south-west.

Westbury Leigh S.W. of Westbury
1316 de Lye 1330 Lye

The name comes from OE *leah*, 'clearing in a wood', in this case the former Forest of SELWOOD. See also LEA.

Westwood S.W. of Bradford
987 Westwuda 1086 Westwode 1285 Westwod 1363 Overwestwode, Netherwestwode

OE *west-wudu*, descriptive of the former stretch of the Forest of SELWOOD which lay to the south-west of Bradford. The 1363 forms are present-day Upper and Lower Westwood.

Wexcombe N.E. of Ludgershall
1155 West Cumbe 1156 Westcumba 1173 Wex Cumba 1201 Wexcumbe 1288 de Woxecumbe 1314 Wexcombe 1426 Waxcombe 1470 Westcombe

Probably OE *west-cumb*, 'westerly valley'. The village lies in a small dry valley to the west of Tidcombe. Or possibly 'wax-valley', denoting a farm whose owner kept bees.

Whaddon S.E. of Salisbury
1086 in Watedene 1109/20 Hwatedena 1242 Watden' 1243 in Waddone 1273 in Watdene 1316 Whaddon

OE *hwæt-denu*, 'valley where the wheat grows or is stored'.

Whaddon S.W. of Melksham
1086 Wadone 1234 Waddune 1253 Waddone 1363 Whadone 1428 Whaddon

OE *wad-dun* or *hwæt-dun*, 'hill where the woad or wheat grows'. Although, as the land here is low and flat, the suffix may be an early corruption of OE *denu*, 'valley'.

Whitbourne W. of Warminster
1249 Whyteborne, Wytteburne Hen.III Hwytburn 1412 Whiteborne

OE *hwitan-burna*, 'white stream', with reference to a small affluent of the River Frome, which is milky because of the chalk soil. Or the first element may be the personal name, *Hwita*.

Whiteparish S.E. of Salisbury
1278 la Whytechyrche 1289 Whitchirche 1298 Album Monasterium 1301 la Whiteparosse 1306 Whyteparisch 1318 of Wyteparosche 1324 la Whiteparisshe 1359 Whiteparys 1487 White Parish

The village is in the White Chalk district, and is probably named after the original chalk-built church here. Confusion between the precise meanings of 'church' and 'parish' seems to be the reason for the present form of the name. *Album Monasterium* is an inaccurate Latin translation of the name.

Whitley N.W. of Melksham
1001 at Witlege 1086 Witelie 1167 Wittelega 1286 Whitlee 1296 Wytelegh 1333 Whytele

OE *hwitan-leah*, 'white meadow or clearing'. Or the first element may be the personal name *Hwita*: see WHITBOURNE.

Wilcot N.W. of Pewsey
940 æt Wilcotum 1086 Wilcote 1279 Welcot 1285 in Wylekote

Either *Willan-cote*, 'Willa's cottages', or *wielle-cote*, 'cottages by the spring or well'. At Wilcot, the Domesday Survey records "a new church, an excellent house and a good vineyard".

Wilsford S.W. of Pewsey
892 Wifeles ford 1086 Wivlesford 1275 Wifleford 1288 Wyllisford 1316 Willesford 1428 Wyvelesford

OE *Wifeles-ford*, 'Wifel's ford'. The ford was on the Avon, either at the end of the lane east of the church, or just south of Cuttenham Farm on the Woodborough road, marking the spot where the parishes of Wilsford, North Newnton and Charlton all meet. Also spelled Willesford during the 19th century.

Wilton
838 Uuilton 854 Wiltun 871 æt Wiltune 955 to Wiltune 962 on Wiltune 1086 de Wiltune, Wiltone

Wylye-tun, 'farmstead on the river Wylye'. The river-name probably comes from the Welsh word *gwili*, 'twisting, turning'. Wilton is situated at the confluence of the Wylye and Nadder rivers, which provided an excellent defensive position for the Saxon *burh* which was established here in the 10th century (see also CHISBURY). Wilton was also a Royal Borough and seat of the first Kings of England. The town gave its name to the county, Wiltshire, and was capital of the shire by the 8th century.

Wilton S.E. of Marlborough
1227 Wulton 1289 Wolton 1327 Woultone 1402 Wilton

OE *wull-tun*, 'farm where wool is prepared or stored'.

Wingfield W. of Trowbridge

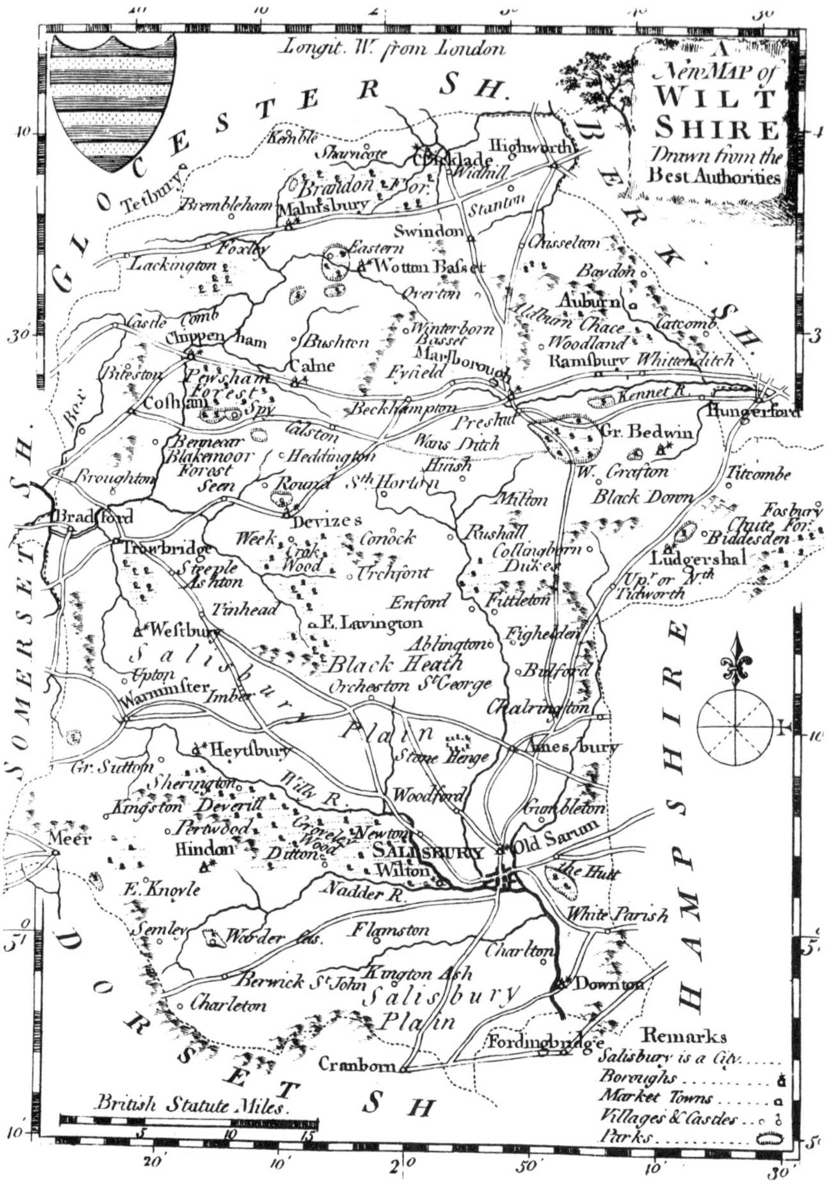

Map of Wiltshire, 1785

954 Wuntfeld 1086 Winefel 1242 Winesfeld 1281 Wynyfeud c1290 Wyneffeld 1316 de Wyncfelde 1428 Wenfeld 1446 Wynfeld

OE *Wines-feld*, 'Wina's open land'. The village is near the former northern edge of the old Forest of Selwood, although the woodland cover had been much reduced by the time of Domesday. The 954 spelling appears corrupt.

Winsley W. of Bradford
1242 Winesleg' 1341 Wynesleye 1362 Winsleigh 1363 Winslegh 1523 Wynnesley

OE *Wines-leah*, 'Wina's meadow or open land', probably incorporating the same personal names as in WINGFIELD.

Winterbourne Bassett S. of Wootton Bassett
1086 Wintreburne, Wintreborne 1249 Wynterburn' Basset 1316 Wynterburne Basset

OE *winter-burna*, 'winter stream or torrent', named after the headwaters of the river Kennet, which gush during the winter months but, upstream from the springs at Swallowhead, are reduced to a trickle during the summer. The stream has also been called the Lambourne. The name 'Winterbourne' is a common one for villages on chalkland streams where the water-table drops considerably in summer; in fact, the name became so widespread during the later Middle Ages that many settlements described as *Wintreburne* in DB were subsequently forced to add suffixes or changes their names completely (eg. SHREWTON) to minimise confusion. The nearby farm of RABSON was formerly known as North Winterbourne, and WINTERBOURNE MONKTON lies two miles to the south. The village is part of the old estate of the *Basset* family, first being owned by Alan Basset in 1194. See also BERWICK BASSETT, COMPTON BASSETT and WOOTTON BASSETT.

Winterbourne Dauntsey N.E. of Salisbury
1086 Wintreburne 1275 Winterburn' Daunteseye 1316 Winterburne Dauntesey

See WINTERBOURNE BASSETT. The river on which the village lies is an affluent of the Salisbury Avon, now simply called the Bourne, and formerly known as *Colinga burn*, after the village of COLLINGBOURNE upstream. Winterbourne Dauntsey stands between WINTERBOURNE EARLS and WINTERBOURNE GUNNER. Roger *Danteseye* held the manor in 1242 and probably came from DAUNTSEY.

Winterbourne Earls N.E. of Salisbury
1086 Wintreburne 1198 Winterburn Comitis Sar' 1281 Wynterburn Lungespeye c1290 Wynt'born Comitis 1323 Eurleswynterbourne 1324 Heorleswynterbourne 1553 Winterbourne Errells

See WINTERBOURNE BASSETT and WINTERBOURNE DAUNTSEY. The manor formerly belonged to the Earls of Lancaster, Lincoln and Salisbury (Latin *comitis*, 'earl or count'). The Earls of Salisbury during the 12th and 13th centuries were members of the *Longspée* family.

Winterbourne Gunner N.E. of Salisbury
1086 Wintreburne 1199 Maiden Winť'borñ 1266 Wintreburn Gunore 1268 Wynterburne Gunnore 1277 Wynterburne Chyreburgh c1290 Wynt'born Cherburg 1314 Maidene Wynterborne 1316 Winterburne Ĝonnor 1332 Winterburne Cherberwe

See WINTERBOURNE BASSETT and WINTERBOURNE DAUNTSEY. *Gunnora* de la Mere held lands here in the 13th century. The 'Maiden' prefix may either be a reference to her or to the parish church, which was dedicated to St Mary in the 12th century. John *de Cherenburgh* held the manor in 1227, and the family name possibly came from the town of Cherbourg in France. The village was also known locally until last century as Cherborough.

Winterbourne Monkton N. of Avebury
1086 Wintrèborne 1249 Winterburne Monachorum 1251 Moneke Wynterburn 1267 Wynterburne Abbatis Glaston' c1290 Wynt'burn Monach' 1316 Wynterborne Monachorum 1348 Monketon 1544 Winterborn Mounckton

On the same stream as WINTERBOURNE BASSETT. The Abbot of Glastonbury was tenant in 1086, the manor having been given to him by Queen Elfrida. *Monachorum* means 'belonging to the monks', referring either to the monastery at Glastonbury or to the small priory which existed at nearby AVEBURY.

Winterbourne Stoke W. of Amesbury
1086 Wintreburnestoch, Wintrebornestoca 1169 Winterburnestoke

See WINTERBOURNE BASSETT. This is the only one of the current Winterbourne villages which had its suffix as early as DB. Winterbourne Stoke is on an affluent of the Wylye, and would originally have gone under the simpler name of Stoke (OE *stoc*, 'stockaded place': see BAVERSTOCK).

Winterslow and **Winterslow, East, Middle, West** E. of Salisbury
1086 Wintresleu, Wintreslei 1166 Winterlawa, Winterlawa Reḡ 1201 Wintreslau 1263 West Winterslewe 1323 of Wyntereslowe 1351 Wyntreslewe Uppinton

OE *Wintran-hlaw*, 'Wintre's mound or burial place'. The suffix on the 1166 form is an abbreviation of Latin *regis*, 'king', a reminder that the manor of Winterslow was once Crown property. *Wyntreslewe Upinton* is the hamlet of East Winterslow which, at over 500 feet, is the highest of the four settlements. Middle Winterslow was also known locally as Middleton.

Wishford, Great and Little N. of Wilton
1086 Wicheford c1190 de Wykeford Majori 1289 Magna Wycheford 1316 Parva Whicheford 1332 Muchelewychford 1351 Muchel Wichford 1428 Magna Wyccheford 1513 Wyssheford Magna

Either OE *wic-ford*, 'dwellig or cottage by the ford', or OE *wice-ford*, 'ford by the wych-elm'. Wych-elms were once prolific along the valleys of Wiltshire but are now less common. The ford over the Wylye probably lay between Great and Little Wishford in the days when the main Wilton-Warminster road crossed the river here. *Magna* ('great') and *Majori* ('greater') are Latin forms, while *Muchel* derives from the OE word *michel*, which has a similar meaning.

Witherington N. of Downton
1086 Widetone 1209 Widintona 1255 Wythiton 1270 Wythetun

Probably OE *withegn-tun*, 'farmstead by the withies', referring to its lowly situation by the Salisbury Avon.

Wolfhall S.E. of Marlborough
1086 Ulfela 1180 Wulfhala 1242 Wlfhale 1249 Wolfehale 1324 Wolphal 1490 Wulfhall

Wulfan-heall, 'Wulfa's hall or palace', or *wulfan-healh*, 'corner of land frequented by wolves'. Wolfhall lay within Savernake Forest, where wolves were common until at least the 14th century. OE *wulf* also occurs in Wulfmere, within the Forest of BRADON.

Woodborough W. of Pewsey
1208 Wideberghe c1220 Wodeberg 1241 in Wudeberg' 1277 Wodebore 1278 Wodebore 1596 Woodborough

Wudu-beorg, 'wooded hill or mound', probably with reference to the prominent and isolated Woodborough Hill which stands just over a mile to the north of the village.

Woodfalls S.E. of Salisbury
1258 Wudefolde 1275 Wudefaude 1289 Wodefeld

OE *wudu-fald*, 'sheep-fold in or by the wood'.

Woodford, Lower, Middle and **Upper** N. of Salisbury
972 wuduforda 1120 Wodeford c1250 Wodeford Major 1279 Netherwodeford 1316 Woodeford Magna, Wodeford Parva 1332 Wodeford Minor 1422 Litelwodeford 1524 Upwodford 1525 Grete Woodford, Lytle Woodford

OE *wudu-ford*, 'ford by the wood', or possibly 'ford made of wood'. As there are many crossing-places over the Salisbury Avon, it is difficult to pinpoint the site of the original ford: possibly there were formerly fords in each village. Upper and Lower Woodford were cnce known as Great and Little (or Nether) Woodford respectively. The suffixes describe the villages' relative positions on the Avon.

Wootton Bassett (ootton)
680 Wdetun 844 Wttune 983 Wudetunnincga gemære 1086 Wodetone 1229 Wutton 1272 Wotton Bassett 1315 Bassetteswotton 1502 Olde Wotton

Wudu-tun, 'enclosure or farmstead in the wood', ie. BRADON Forest. There is still a Wood Street in the town, which formerly led towards Bradon. The 983 form refers to 'the boundary of the people of Wootton'. Alan *Basset* acquired the manor in the early 13th century (see also WINTERBOURNE BASSETT). Known locally as 'Bassett'.

Wootton Rivers (ootton) S. of Marlborough
804 Wdutun 1086 Otone 1212 Wotton c1290 de Wottone 1332 Wotton Ryvers 1371 Wutton Ryveyrs 1428 Wotton Ryver 1490 Wutton Ryver

Wudu-tun, 'enclosure or farmstead in the wood', ie. SAVERNAKE Forest. Walter *de Riperia* held the manor in 1212.

Worton (wurtun) S.W. of Devizes
1173 Wrton, Wrtona 1195 Wurton 1220 Worton

Possibly OE *wyrt-tun*, 'herb enclosure', although Longstaff suggests that it is a corruption of *ufer-tun*, 'upper enclosure'. Or the first element may be OE *weorth*: see HIGHWORTH.

Wraxhall, North (rocksall) N.W. of Corsham
1086 Werocheshalle 1229 Wrokeshale, Wraxhal' 1281 de Worxhale 1468 Northworxhall

Wrocces-heall, 'Wrocca's hall', or *wrocces-healh*, 'corner of land frequented by buzzards'. 'North' to distinguish from WRAXHALL, SOUTH.

Wraxhall, South N. of Bradford
1227 Wroxhal 1242 Wrokeshal' c1290 Wrockeshale 1316 de Wroxhale 1468 Suthwroxhall

See WRAXHALL, NORTH.

Wroughton (wraughton) S. of Swindon
c890 Ellendun 1086 Elendune, Wertune, in Wervetone c1100 Eallandun 1196 Worftun 1226 Werktun 1242 Worefton 1270 Elendone quod est Worftone 1279 Overe Werfton 1291 Elindone 1300 Wrfton 1365 Warghton 1428 Wroghton, Over Worston, Nethyr Wrofton 1620 Wroughton al. Elingdon

OE *woerc-tun*, 'farmstead on the River Worf', which was the old name for the Ray: there is still a Wharf Road in the village. Wroughton was formerly made up of six manors: *Salthorpe* (SALTHROP), *Elcumbe* (ELCOMBE), *Ellandun, Werveton, Wertone* and *Westlecott*. Ellandun means 'elder-tree down' and was the site of a major battle in 825 when Egbert, King of the West Saxons, beat Beornwulf, King of Mercia, on the downs above Markham Bottom. The battle took place near the parish church, which significantly is surrounded by the vestiges of earthworks and is dedicated to St John & St Helen. Known as Ellendune Church until the 19th century, it lies directly on the former boundaries of Ellandun and Elcombe. St Helen seems to be connected with the *ellan-* element in the old name, which possibly signifies a pre-Christian goddess or river-spirit (ie. Ellan). The name of Ellandun possibly went out of currency because of superstitions about the elder-tree's bad luck, stemming from its alleged use for forming the Cross upon which Christ died. *Wervtone*, otherwise Nether Wroughton, is equivalent to the nucleus of the present-day village. *Wertone*, or Over Wroughton, is present-day Overtown or Overton, situated on the scarp-top to the south of the village.

Wylye (wily)
688 Wileo (flumen) *880/5 æt Welig* *901 Biwilig* *943 wilig* *1086 Wilgi, Wili* *c1190 Wyly* *1268 Wyly Abbatisse* *1378 Wylgy*

The forms prior to the Domesday Survey refer to the river Wylye, which name is of Celtic origin, possibly derived from *gwili*, 'tricky stream', or Welsh *gwy*, 'flood or water'. The river subsequently gave its name to the village of Wylye, also to WILTON and, indirectly, to the county, Wiltshire. Wylye was a holding of the Abbess of Wilton.

Yarnfield N. of Mere
1086 Gernefelle *1232 Jernefeld* *1260 Gernefeud* *c1400 Yarnefeld* *1402 Yernefeld*

Possibly OE *earnen-feld*, 'eagle's field', although the first element, *Gerne*, may denote an OE stream-name.

Yatesbury E. of Calne
1086 Etesberie *1199 Hyatesbir̃* *1222 Jetebur* *1226 Getesbir* *1239 Yetesbur* *1249 Ytesbyr'* *c1290 Ietesbury, Yattesbur'* *1324 Yatesbury*

Probably OE *gat-berie*, 'open field where the goats are kept'. The Rev. A.C. Smith once described Yatesbury as "one of the smallest, humblest and most retired parishes on the Wiltshire Downs".

Yatton Keynell N.W. of Chippenham
1086 Etone, Getone *1242 de Yattone* *1245 Jettun'* *1258 Iatton* *1317 of Iattone Kayngnel* *1334 Yetton Caynel* *1530 Churcheyatton*

Possibly OE *geat-tun*, 'farmstead by the gate or gap': the village is at the head of a valley which leads westwards to By Brook. The knight Henry *Caynel* had a holding here in 1242. *Churcheyatton* distinguishes the larger village from the hamlet of West Yatton.

Zeals W. of Mere
956 at Seale *1086 Sele, Sela* *1176 Seles* *1264 Celes* *1302 Seeles* *1428 Selesaylesbury* *1495 Netherseals* *1502 Selyscleverdon* *1571 both Sealles*

Either OE *sele, selas,* 'house, dwelling', or OE*sealh,* 'willow, sally'. The manor was granted in 1292 to Walter *de Ailesbury*. The *Clevedons*, another local family, have their family arms in Mere church. Hoare records two manors (hence: *both Sealles*): "Seals Ailesbury or Over Zeals; Seals Clevedon or Nether Zeals". The latter location is Zeals House which lies towards Mere.